NATURAL DOG CARE

NATURAL DOG CARE

ALTERNATIVE THERAPIES FOR DOG HEALTH AND VITALITY

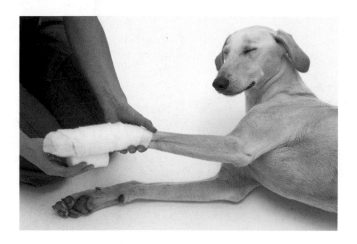

A complete guide with over 270 practical photographs

John Hoare
BVSc MRCVS VetMFHom

Photography by Jane Burton

LORENZ BOOKS

This edition is published by Lorenz Books
an imprint of Anness Publishing Ltd
Blaby Road, Wigston
Leicestershire LE18 4SE
info@anness.com

www.lorenzbooks.com
www.annesspublishing.com

If you like the images in this book and would
like to investigate using them for publishing,
promotions or advertising, please visit our website
www.practicalpictures.com for more information.

© Anness Publishing Ltd 2013

A CIP catalogue record for this book
is available from the British Library.

Publisher: Joanna Lorenz
Project Editor: Sarah Ainley
Photographer: Jane Burton
Illustrator: Anna Koska
Copy Editor: Raje Airey
Cover Design: Nigel Partridge
Designer: Lisa Tai
Production Controller: Mai-Ling Collyer

ADDITIONAL PHOTOGRAPHY
t=top; b=bottom; l=left; r=right
John Daniels p17 cutouts, p18b, p25b, p26t and b, p57t,
p69bl, p73t and b, p78b, p81b, p86b, p87t, p95; Life File
p14t; Michelle Garrett p58t, p59tl and tr; Kim Taylor p9t,
pp12–13, 15b.

Contents

Introduction

When internal energies are able to circulate smoothly and
freely, and the energy of the mind is not scattered, but it is
focused and concentrated, illness and disease can be avoided.

The Yellow Emperor's Classic of Medicine, 250BC

The philosophy of harmony and balance

The underlying philosophy of all known complementary therapies is one of harmony and balance. Humans and animals alike should be at one with the world, with nature and with one another.

This philosophy recognizes that there is more to life than the material element that we learn about from our five senses. Living things are believed to have mental and spiritual bodies as well as the physical body that modern medicine is based upon. True health can only exist when all three bodies, mental, spiritual and physical, are healthy and in balance with each other, and the totality is in harmony with the world.

Scientists can be reluctant to contemplate the existence of things which they cannot measure. Yet how should one measure love and hate, or good and evil, for example? Does this mean that emotions do not exist and spirituality is a delusion? Yet if they do exist, where do they exist? Perhaps there are invisible mental and emotional bodies that co-exist in time and space with the more-easily measured physical body?

Kirlian photography demonstrates that the electromagnetic field of the physical body extends beyond its physical form. Some people believe this to be a reflection of the body's "aura". Sequential Kirlian images have been taken during holistic treatment sessions. These show that the aura becomes larger and more well-defined as the session goes on. Perhaps in time, equipment will be developed that would measure the body's electromagnetic field, to determine how it differs from one in a state of optimum health. If it could feed back a "vibration" to harmonize the basic electromagnetic vibrations of the body, it could initiate a healing process. However, for the moment this is unlikely to happen: the medical profession is concerned only with trying to understand in detail how the physical body works and to a large extent ignores the effects that the invisible bodies have upon the physical one.

In a culture which accepts that a living organism has a totality greater than the sum of its parts, and in which all life is interdependent, the terms health and disease take on differing shades of meaning. In most dictionaries health is defined in terms of soundness of the body and illness as an unhealthy state of the body. Disease is seen in terms of illnesses of the body and sometimes the mind. Thus, health and disease are defined in terms of each other: good health is an absence of bad health, illness or disease.

In holistic terms good health is a natural result of being completely at one with the world, in a state of ease. When this sublime state is broken, a state of dis-ease is created in which mental and physical abnormalities can develop. Consequently, a state of good health or well-being demands that one's environment is suited to one's lifestyle and basic physical needs.

The need for environmental compatibility is just as valid for animals as for humans. When you undertake to keep a dog as a pet, you artificially restrict its interaction with nature and the world. This means that you become responsible for providing the dog with the wherewithal to lead a healthy life. In return, if the relationship is properly developed, you will be rewarded by the pleasure the dog can give you and the lessons in living and loving that it can help you to learn.

Your dog's needs are very similar to yours. Although they may vary in detail, the basic requirements are the same: a dog needs good habitation, sanitation, and nutrition. It needs to exercise if its physical body is to remain healthy, and it needs protection from prolonged or excessive stress. Above all, it needs to be in a good, healthy, loving relationship. Love is the one universally recognized foundation for good health. The aim of this book is to help you achieve that state for your dog.

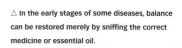

△ **In the early stages of some diseases, balance can be restored merely by sniffing the correct medicine or essential oil.**

△ CLOCKWISE **Fit and healthy dogs need as much exercise as we do. If it can be combined with pleasurable activity and owner involvement, all the better. Do remember though that all pleasure has to be paid for. A gambol in the sea will need to be** followed by a drying and grooming session on returning home. There may well be knots and tangles to comb out of the hair, and mud to be removed from both the coat and from between the toes. Remember also to examine your dog for early signs of pains or strains after bouts of prolonged or violent exercise. Check the dog over for minor injuries where treatment or medication may be needed; a massage is always a good way to relax the dog.

Good health in dogs

A fit and healthy dog in the prime of life is a wonderful animal. Like humans a dog's life proceeds through several stages. First there is the "infant" or puppy, dependent upon its mother. It has to be weaned and taught how to live in a social group. Very quickly the puppy grows and becomes an extremely active "adolescent", or young adult dog. Mature adulthood follows, and gradually the dog becomes old. In time it will follow natural laws and die.

The basic physical needs of a dog remain the same throughout its life. The fine details vary according to the stage of development that the dog has reached and the life that both the dog and its owner lead. Young, active dogs need a lot more exercise and a different food ration from that of a more elderly dog, for example.

Humans have had a direct impact on dogs as a species. Selective breeding over the centuries has led to the production of hundreds of different dog breeds, each with its own preferred conformation. Each breed has its own basic requirements, and these can be very specific. Accommodation that is suitable for a very small dog, such as a Dachshund is obviously wrong for a larger breed, such as a St Bernard. The two breeds also have different dietary requirements,

△ The more elderly dog is often content to sit in peace and comfort, in a quiet corner of the garden, to enjoy the warmth of the sun and simply watch the world go by.

mainly in the amount of food they need to eat every day, but also in its composition.

Fit, healthy dogs of all breeds and ages share certain characteristics. Their coats are in good condition and do not smell. Their eyes are bright and there are no stains on their faces from tear overspill. There is no discharge from their ears or nose, and no smell from their ears. They move freely and easily and do not limp. They can enjoy strenuous exercise without physical distress at normal temperatures for a time commensurate with their breed and age.

The breeding patterns that have emphasized characteristics of many of today's breeds have sometimes inadvertently encouraged susceptibility to specific diseases. Genetically

◁ Fit puppies are very active. They need robust toys to help the development of the teeth and jaws, and to divert their destructive impulses.

programmed susceptibility to disease cannot be eliminated unless there is a change in the criteria for selecting breeding stock, although there are screening programmes currently in place to identify those animals susceptible to inherited disease, in order to minimize the risks.

While conventional veterinary medicine is used to treat the physical symptoms of a sick animal, holistic care is interested in the whole dog, and in preventing disease occuring. Providing a dog with a lifestyle suited to his physical and emotional needs will stimulate his body's ability to heal itself: optimum health is always the best possible protection against disease.

Holistic medicine

Modern science tends to concentrate on understanding the world by looking at each of its components in great detail. This approach has been taken up by the medical professions, and medical and veterinary specialists concentrate their attention on the minutiae of their patient's physical symptoms, sometimes to the exclusion of everything else. Drugs are chosen for their effect on the system or the tissue thought to be the source of the illness. Problems caused by the drugs appearing in other parts of the body are seen as inevitable side effects which have to be tolerated. All patients are expected to respond to treatment in the same way and there is little allowance made for individuality.

Holistic medicine, both human and veterinary, takes a much wider view of the patient and their disease. In holistic medicine, the three components that make up the individual – the spiritual, mental and physical – are all considered to have a bearing on the development of disease and are taken into account when planning the treatment. The patient is very much an individual and the treatment must take account of their unique needs. This is often expressed as "treating the patient and not the disease". There are difficulties involved

△ **Physiotherapy can help control pain and speed healing in injured tissues, and is an important part of both conventional and holistic care.**

in holistic care for dogs in that the vet is not able to discuss emotions and moral concepts with the patient. However, in the same way that a doctor looks to the parent for information when treating a young child, so the vet will seek imput from the dog's owner.

Because no one therapy is 100 per cent effective in all cases, more than one therapy, or more than one therapist, may be needed. It is imperative that the vet and all therapists

involved explain their own therapy, and how it is expected to interact with others: aromatherapy can inhibit the action of homeopathic remedies, for example, while massage is compatible with all therapies.

Holistic medicine does not aim to ignore conventional science but to work alongside it in a supportive role. Complementary treatments can promote well-being in a fit and healthy dog and can help to alleviate the distress of illness, but if modern drugs are needed for acute cases of disease, then they are given. The prime concern with any form of veterinary care is always how it will affect the quality of the dog's life.

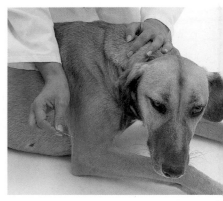

△ **Contrary to expectations, most dogs are not afraid of the acupuncture needle. They lie still and relaxed while the needles are inserted.**

◁ **Dogs always enjoy a simple massage session, since it means they get their tummies tickled.**

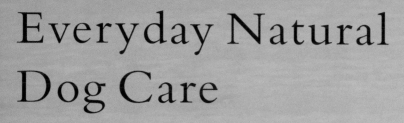

Everyday Natural Dog Care

From ancient times it has been recognized that there is an intimate relationship

between the activity and life of animals and their natural environment.

The Yellow Emperor's Classic of Medicine, 250BC

Responsible dog ownership

Dogs can be extremely good companions, but they can also be a great liability, and if their physical and mental needs are not properly met, the relationship between dog and owner can be disastrous.

The basic error is to think that a dog is human and not canine. The physical needs of a dog are similar to those of a human: food, water and suitable accommodation are the minimum requirement for keeping a dog in health. Dogs can show behaviour (and disease) patterns that indicate they have emotions similar to those felt and acted on by humans, but this does not make them the same as us. At all times they remain dogs: they rationalize less and react more to natural instinct, and they are much more physical creatures than humans.

Dogs are social animals and in nature they live in packs. The pack has a social structure. It is led by the bravest, strongest male dog for the length of time that he can dominate or beat all the other dogs in fair fight. The pack leader has first choice of everything: food, mates and resting place. When you choose a canine companion you adopt the role of pack leader, and it is essential that this is understood by your dog. You do not have to physically fight with the dog to establish your superiority, but you must be able to convince it that you are superior, and that its place in the pack is below that of every human. Having established

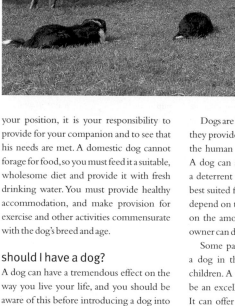

◁ A working dog would usually be trained as a pup. Collies are active dogs with a strong herding instinct and they make ideal sheep dogs.

your position, it is your responsibility to provide for your companion and to see that his needs are met. A domestic dog cannot forage for food, so you must feed it a suitable, wholesome diet and provide it with fresh drinking water. You must provide healthy accommodation, and make provision for exercise and other activities commensurate with the dog's breed and age.

should I have a dog?

A dog can have a tremendous effect on the way you live your life, and you should be aware of this before introducing a dog into your home. There are organizations which provide a questionnaire that can help you decide if you want a dog and if so, which breeds would best fit into your lifestyle. A vet could tell you more about this. Examine your reasons for wanting a dog: most of all remember that you are not being fair on either yourself or the dog if you are unable to accept your duty as a dog owner.

◁ Dogs of all ages love to play, yet this need for interactive games is often neglected by owners with hectic lives of their own.

Dogs are kept as pets in the home because they provide companionship, and can fulfill the human need to give and receive love. A dog can also act as a burglar alarm and a deterrent to intruders. The breed of dog best suited for the role of house pet should depend on the house size and location and on the amount of time and attention the owner can devote to the dog.

Some parents feel that the presence of a dog in the home is valuable for their children. A well-trained dog can prove to be an excellent companion and playmate. It can offer the children protection while giving them opportunities for learning the responsibilities of looking after a dependant being, learning about reproduction, and the emotional lessons of life, involving love, death and grief. A small or medium breed of dog is probably the most appropriate for young children.

Working dogs are chosen for more specific criteria. Livestock farmers need dogs with a strong herding instinct and ability, while hunters choose dogs that can retrieve game or hunt vermin: Collies and the gundog breeds are ideal in this context. Dogs can also be a blessing for some blind people. Hearing dogs are trained to help people who are deaf, and helping dogs are trained to help those with severe physical handicaps. These dogs are highly trained by experts, and the potential owner is then trained to work with the dog.

the cost of having a dog

As soon as you accept a dog into your home you become entirely responsible for its well-being. This commitment will make demands upon your resources in terms of money, time and space.

The financial cost of a dog can vary from a nominal sum for a mongrel or a dog from a charity or rescue society to the expense of a pedigree dog. The ongoing costs include feeding (the larger the breed, the more it will eat) and vet's fees. The latter will include initial and on-going vaccinations, while treatments for sickness and injury should also be budgeted for. Pet insurance will help here, although there is usually an excess fee per incident to be paid, and the price of premiums rises every year.

In addition, kennelling fees may be needed for holiday periods. The quarantine regulations in some European countries are now being eased, but along with dog passports there is the cost of rabies testing and vaccinations, and the cost of identity chipping, which involves injecting a tiny silicon capsule between the dog's shoulders or behind its ears. The chip acts like an invisible barcode and is read to reveal the identity of the dog – its name, its owner's details, and its vaccination history.

◁ Older children and dogs make ideal companions. When they grow up together, they form a very special bond that will usually last a lifetime.

Dogs who live in the home need to be trained but the time commitment of dog training is considerable. Toilet training a puppy may take up to six months and it can be tedious and inconvenient. For older puppies, an hour a week at a dog-training class will teach the owner how to train the dog. Ideally this should be supplemented by half an hour a day of informal training at home. Time must also be found for giving the dog attention in the form of play and free-running exercise. The amount needed varies but dogs from working breeds need at least one hour every day. Inactive dogs soon become bored and unhealthy.

Space is another important factor. The dog needs its own place to sleep and feed and these must come from your house or garden. You may have to travel to find a space for your dog to exercise, and this will involve spending more time with the dog.

The next decision is whether to buy a puppy or an adult dog. If buying a puppy you must allow yourself time to train it. Ideally, puppies should be rehomed as soon as possible after seven weeks to allow for good socialization with humans and other dogs. Rehoming a pup after 13 weeks can lead to behavioural troubles because the puppy has not learned how to react with others. Some breeders are reluctant to part with pups before they are fully vaccinated at 10–12 weeks old.

If buying an adult dog, find out all you can about why the dog is being rehomed. There will usually be a tense time while the dog comes to terms with its new situation, but if it is being rehomed for behavioural reasons, especially if the dog shows signs of aggressive behaviour, then it is best to leave well alone. Retraining is difficult and potentially dangerous for anyone without experience of handling disturbed dogs.

◁ Regular free-running exercise is important to keep a dog in fitness. Woodland runs are a particular favourite, but they can be hard to come by for dogs living in built-up areas.

Housing your dog

Having decided that you want a dog, the next thing to decide is where it is going to live, eat and sleep. Most dogs tend to live with the family inside the house. Before you get the dog, all members of the household must agree which parts of the house it will be allowed in. It is best to keep the dog out of the bedrooms. This is for two main reasons: the first is hygiene – think of fleas and worms. Secondly, in nature the top dog gets the choice of sleeping accommodation. Allowing the dog access to your sleeping space can be the start of it thinking that it is superior to you. It is surprising how many people report that their dog, once granted the privilege of access to the bed by one partner, begins to object to the other partner getting into it. It may mean fitting a stair-gate to stop the dog from going upstairs.

the dog's bed

If the dog is to be housed in the home, it should have its own bed or basket that can be easily cleaned if it gets stained. This may be of plastic, or a lined basket. Open wicker baskets are difficult to clean if they get badly soiled. Doggy bean bags are also

suitable, but you will need a spare cover for when accidents occur. The bed will require bedding that can be cleaned from time to time. There are several proprietary materials available now that allow fluids to pass through while the top remains dry. These make ideal linings. Blankets and rugs can be used but they will require constant washing, and need to be replaced frequently. The bed itself should not be in the main room of the house. If you have a conservatory (porch), that is probably the best place.

△ Veterinary bedding is probably the most hygienic type of bedding available. Wherever he sleeps, your dog will appreciate a soft warm covering to lie on.

The bed may be kept in the kitchen provided there is space for it to be kept away from the food-preparing areas. If the dog's bed has to be kept in the main room, it should be in a quiet place where it is inconspicuous, and where the dog can retreat to it and be out of the way when necessary.

kennelling

If there is no suitable place in the house to put the bed, there is no reason why the dog should not be provided with a suitable kennel for resting and sleeping. The main requirements are that the kennel should be big enough for the dog to enter easily, stand up in and turn around in. Think in terms of it being at least one-and-a-half dogs high, one-and-a-half dogs wide and one-dog long. The door should be large enough for the dog to get inside without injury and should face away from the prevailing wind.

◁ A plastic basket makes a practical choice for a dog's bed because it is easy to keep clean. It will need some kind of soft rug or mat, however, to make it comfortable and cosy.

◁ An outdoor kennel should be kept dry and sheltered as best as possible. Line the floor and add a rug or mat for warmth and comfort. Fresh water should be available at all times.

If the kennel can be situated so that the door is sheltered by another structure, so much the better. The whole kennel must be weatherproof. A strong wooden crate with a sloping roof covered with good-quality roofing felt is sufficient. The front should be hinged or removable so that the inside of the kennel can be cleaned and disinfected when needed. The floor needs to be raised off the ground sufficiently to prevent damp coming in. This can be done by standing the kennel on bricks or fitting it with short, stout legs. Alternatively, the bed could be placed in a suitable outbuilding. If the building is very big, it might be better to put a kennel inside it to give the dog a sense of his own private space.

Kennel bedding is needed for comfort. Again, special animal bedding materials are the best to use. Most dogs are better adapted to living in colder conditions than humans (for a start they have their own personal fur coats), and it is surprising how much heat is given off by the dog's body and retained within the kennel. A healthy kennelled dog should only need extra bedding in the very worst weather conditions; these are usually damp winter winds and heavy driving rain, sleet and snow. Cold weather on its own is not a particular problem, unless the temperature is well below freezing.

▽ Doggy bean bags are extremely comfortable, but while some dogs can't live without theirs, others just can't be persuaded to try them.

△ Thick travel rugs are useful to line baskets or for the dog to lie down on when travelling in the car.

▷ A collapsable travelling cage has many uses at home or away. Fitted with a waterproof lining, a soft rug, fresh water and a few toys, it becomes the dog's personal retreat wherever he is.

Feeding your dog

A fully-grown dog only needs one good meal a day. If fresh or canned food is fed, a rough guide is 15g (½oz) of food per 450g (1lb) of body weight. Pups and young dogs need to be fed more often: four meals a day at three months, three meals at four months, and two meals at 5–7 months. Fresh drinking water, preferably filtered or spring, should be available at all times.

The dog needs to have its own eating place. Dogs should never be fed from the table, but should wait until the family has eaten. They should have their own food and water utensils which should be washed separately from the rest of the family's things. Glazed earthenware or stainless steel bowls are preferable to plastic ones as toxic chemicals may leach out into the food.

◁ Active dogs use more energy than inactive ones and need to eat more calories. If your dog is gaining weight, cut out calorie-rich treats before reducing the size of its main meal, then increase the amount of exercise.

home-made diets

It is possible to devise a vegetarian diet for a dog, but the dog is not a natural vegetarian and it's digestive system is poorly adapted to coping with it, so it is not recommended. The most nutritious of home-made diets is probably the Billinghurst diet. This is based on the recommendations of an Australian vet, Dr Billinghurst, and consists of raw,

◁ Obviously this pair will need different rations, although pound for pound, the smaller Chihuahua will need more food than the Doberman.

meaty bones combined with puréed green vegetables and over-ripe fruit. The diet closely resembles the natural diet of a dog in the wild: when the pack kills an animal, its abdomen is opened and the contents of its paunch are eaten first. This is semi-fermented vegetable matter – matched by the puréed greens and the over-ripe fruit of the Billinghurst diet. After the paunch, the meat is eaten and the bones are gnawed.

The most economical way of providing this diet today is to feed raw chicken wings with puréed greens and fruit. A dog is quite capable of chewing up raw chicken wings without getting an obstruction. Raw bones are crushable and easy to chew. They will be digested and they contain valuable minerals, vitamins and cartilage

components. However, cooked animal bones are extremely dangerous and should *never* be fed to a dog. They are brittle and crack easily, which means that the dog can easily swallow large pieces of bone which may cause an obstruction. The bone most often removed by vets from dogs' intestines is a cooked chop bone.

If using the Billinghurst diet, feed two-thirds meaty bones to one-third purée. The purée can be poured over the bones or it can be fed separately. If changing from a commercial diet, make the change slowly to give the dog's bowel flora time to adjust.

commercial diets

The animal foodstuff industry produces convenience foods for dogs. A range of products is available to cater specifically for puppies, growing dogs, adult dogs and elderly, lethargic dogs as well as normal healthy ones. These foods are designed to retain their nutritional status over long periods and this enables bulk-buying on a monthly trip to the supermarket. The foods are scientifically prepared to meet the nutritional requirements of different types of dogs in terms of carbohydrates, proteins, fats, vitamins and minerals.

after-dinner
teeth-cleaning
chews

canned
meat-based
feed

all-in-one
complete
feed

dry kibble feed

semi-moist feed

Commercial foods come in three basic forms: canned, semi-moist and dry. Canned foods come in two types. Firstly, there is the all-in-one food, where the contents include the recommended carbohydrate allowance and need no supplementation at all. Secondly, there are those which are mainly meat and are designed to be fed in conjunction with a biscuit supplement. If you feed canned foods, read the labels to make sure that you only supplement those foods that need it.

Semi-moist foods come as processed sausages. These look like large salamis and are usually an all-in-one feed. The dry feeds come as either a biscuit or a kibble. They have several advantages. They store well, with little smell, even when the sack has been opened, provided that it remains dry. Because they do not contain water, they weigh less per meal than canned food, making them cheaper for the manufacturer to transport, and so cheaper to buy.

It is perfectly acceptable to feed a dog a commercial diet, but it is essential that the diet is fed as suggested by the manufacturer. However, the amount of food given to the dog should be that which the dog needs, not that which is suggested on the packet.

Manufacturer's recommendations are on the generous side so that large active dogs are not underfed. Small, lethargic dogs may get too much food and become fat.

Although commercial diets do meet the dog's nutritional requirements, the quality may not be as high as you would expect. The use of meatstuffs unfit for human consumption is banned in the UK but not in many other countries, including the United States. Animal protein can include reclaimed protein from parts of the animal that a human would not willingly eat.

supplements

Dietary supplements are not needed by fit dogs. Your vet will advise you if your dog is sick and a supplement is needed. If you must give one to a healthy dog then choose either *Vitamin B complex* (Brewer's yeast) or *Evening Primrose Oil*.

△ Commercial diets come in many forms. All are designed to contain the dog's normal daily requirement of minerals and vitamins when fed according to the manufacturer's instructions.

▽ If given the choice, dogs would prefer the Billinghurst diet of raw meaty bones and puréed fruit and vegetables.

Exercising your dog

Dogs need regular exercise as much as humans. It helps to keep the heart healthy and promotes good circulation. It keeps muscle tone firm and helps to prevent obesity and premature ageing.

Exercise must be tailored to the age and breed of dog. Young adult Collies can run for a long time and ideally need two hours of exercise a day. This can be tied in with a period of training which helps to keep them mentally alert. Gun dogs, such as Retrievers and Labradors, enjoy strenuous exercise, although labradors are prone to obesity and lethargy. Hounds and terriers that hunt by scent can be difficult to get out of hedgerows and into proper exercise. With this type of dog you may need to devise chasing games to get them into a trot. The smaller breeds, such as Yorkies and Maltese terriers, should not be treated as living toys. They too need periods of strenuous exercise, which may be shorter than those needed by the large breeds, but will keep the dog fit, give it an interest in life, help to prevent obesity and lengthen its lifespan.

Exercise an overweight dog with care. Dogs can tear the ligaments in their stifles (knees) if they twist when their weight is on one leg. This is most common

△ Fit, healthy dogs are always eager for free-running over open grassland. Chasing games give exercise without unduly tiring the owner.

in middle-aged, obese dogs, so if you are trying to slim an overweight dog with exercise, start with something brisk and steady. Do not encourage rigorous activity until the dog's weight has been reduced.

game safety

When playing chasing and fetching games avoid using sticks and tennis balls. It may seem unlikely, but every now and again a dog will misjudge the flight or position of the stick, and the stick then jams into the tissue at the back of its throat or under its tongue. This is painful for the dog, and becomes a job for the vet who will need to anaesthetize the dog, clean the wound and repair any damage.

Splinters of wood can break off the end of a stick and remain in the wounds after the main piece has been removed. Splinters are not always visible, they do not show up on an X-ray, and if left behind in the wound they can lead to further problems. Even tiny splinters will eventually cause a large painful swelling under the jaw or the underside of the neck, which is nature's way of getting rid of penetrating foreign bodies. If such a swelling develops, it means another operation to open the swelling and remove the abnormal tissue. The wound will heal eventually, but it takes time and money, and the whole experience is best avoided.

Misjudgement of the bounce of a tennis ball can result in the dog failing to grasp the ball with its teeth. The ball goes to the back of the dog's mouth, jamming in its throat and obstructing the windpipe. This is an emergency situation. The ball must be removed quickly if the dog is not to suffocate, but this is immensely difficult for the owner out exercising a dog in open country. It is often impossible to get a firm grip on the ball, and a vet may be needed to make an emergency incision in the windpipe (tracheotomy) to get behind the ball so that it can be pushed forwards out of the dog's mouth.

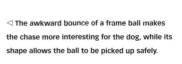

◁ The awkward bounce of a frame ball makes the chase more interesting for the dog, while its shape allows the ball to be picked up safely.

△ Frisbees will give both dog and owner hours of fun. Do not use with overweight dogs as jumping and twisting can damage stifle joints.

suitable toys

It is possible to buy toys for dogs to chase after and to catch safely when exercising outdoors. For dogs that like catching games, frisbees are a good choice. They are too big to stick in the mouth or throat and are soft enough not to damage the dog's teeth if the catch is missed. Dumb-bells can be bought for dogs that like retrieving. The large ends prevent it from entering the dog's mouth. They also keep the bar off the ground which allows the dog to pick it up more easily. Frame balls, which are three curved pieces of strong, brightly coloured plastic joined to make an almost spherical shaped object, are another good choice. These toys bounce unevenly and are said to mimic the running pattern of rabbits, which makes them highly appealing to dogs. Again, they are easy for dogs to pick up and carry, which is something that many dogs love to do when out walking.

△ Swimming is an excellent form of exercise for dogs. It helps all muscle groups and can be especially helpful as a form of physiotherapy after orthopaedic operations.

Daily grooming

A good grooming session should be part of the daily routine. It is good for the dog's coat and gives the owner time to check over the dog's body for any abnormalities. It helps to bring owner and dog closer together whilst the simple action of stroking the dog can help relieve stress in both dog and owner. It is good to incorporate a short massage session with grooming for similar reasons.

The amount of brushing and combing needed depends on the type of coat that the dog has. Smooth, short-coated dogs need regular brushing only. Those with longer or more wiry coats may need combing and a stronger brush. If the coat is very muddy, rinse the worst off, leave the rest to dry and then comb or brush the dry hair. If it is necessary to wash the dog for hygiene or medical purposes, rinse its coat thoroughly unless you have been told by the vet to let any medication dry on its coat. When the shampoo has been well rinsed off, you can towel-dry the coat. If you are blow-drying the dog, do not have the drier too hot or overdry its coat.

◁ Different types of brushes and combs are produced, each with a different use. Select the correct one for your dog's coat to get the best results.

daily grooming routine

Begin with the dog's feet. Clean off any mud and check the feet for balling of hair. In summertime look for any grass awns that may have lodged in the coat. These will penetrate the skin if they are not removed. Grass awns are a common cause of cysts between a dog's toes. When you are cleaning muddy feet, do not forget to check the creases between the toes and also those between the pads of the feet. Mud can ball up in those spaces and result in lameness or superficial infections.

Next, go over the dog starting at its head. Check the hair surrounding its eyes, and clean away any discharges. If there are persistent discharges or the surface of the eye looks discoloured, take the dog to the vet. Do the same with its ears and check that there is no unhealthy smell from them. Grass awns have a liking for ears and eyes as well as feet, so in the summertime check for those as well.

Clean round the dog's mouth, and check the grooves on the side of the lips, especially in dogs with a long coat. If there is an unhealthy smell from its mouth, check for bad teeth, ulcers or foreign material – such as pieces of yesterday's meal – which may be stuck between the teeth. If you are not sure what you

should be looking for, your vet will be able to give you a leaflet showing photographs of healthy and diseased mouths.

If there is a build-up of tartar on the dog's teeth, try feeding raw, meaty bones, teeth-cleaning chews, or tooth brushing using a toothbrush and toothpaste designed for dogs. If no improvement is seen, there may be an internal problem. Your vet may suggest blood tests and a tooth descale under a general anaesthetic.

Next, brush and comb the dog down its back, along the sides and down its legs. While you are doing this look at the skin in general, watching out for any cuts and surface injuries and removing any other grass awns at the same time. Look out for early signs of skin disease in the form of excessive scurf or grease in the coat, spots or pimples. Notice any lumps or bumps. They may be innocuous but if they grow slowly or worry you, you should get them checked out by your vet. Painful areas and joints should be checked as well.

△ Finger-brushes are now available to make teeth-cleaning easier; many dogs will not happily accept a toothbrush in their mouths.

◁ Dogs do not need to be shampooed often but if it is necessary, dry the fur off thoroughly with a towel or lightly blow-dry.

Daily grooming

Time spent grooming your dog is never wasted. Establish a grooming routine as early as possible. The younger a dog is when regular grooming is started the more likely it is that he will tolerate and even enjoy it. Most dogs find matted hair as uncomfortable as we do, and grooming does provide a good opportunity to examine the dog.

◁ **1** Brushing removes dirt, dry mud, leaves and twigs from the coat, and by catching tangles early it will prevent thick matts from developing.

▽ **2** Clean around the eyes very gently, carefully removing any build up of matter in the corner of the eye. In some long-haired breeds, it may be necessary to trim some of the surrounding hairs away.

◁ **3** It may be necessary to pluck hair from the ear canal in long-haired dogs such as Collies, Poodles and Spaniels. In all breeds, excess wax should be cleaned away, and if it looks or smells nasty, see a vet.

△ **4** Don't forget to check the mouth for the build-up of tartar on the teeth. If there is a strong smell check for splinters of meat bone or wood that may have become jammed between the teeth.

Toilet-training puppies

It is impossible to have a good relationship with an untrained dog. Dogs start to learn how to interact with other dogs as early as 4–8 weeks. They learn how to socialize with humans between 5–10 weeks, and how to explore and familiarize themselves with new territory and strange phenomena between 5–16 weeks. They will begin to develop a preference for the type of material on which to deposit their faeces and urine at eight weeks. This means that the best time to get a new puppy is when it is about 7–8 weeks old.

House-training and simple obedience training can begin as soon as a puppy is rehomed because it is at an age when it learns easily and needs to be experiencing as many new things as possible. Delayed exposure to new experiences can impair the pup's development in many ways.

◁ Start training your new puppy as soon as you get him home. He will learn quickest between 7 and 12 weeks of age.

reward training

It is not abnormal for a puppy to be around six months old before it is fully house-trained. The basis of all training should be reward and not punishment. Praise and treats should be given immediately after the dog has done what you wanted it to do correctly. They should be used as a reward for good behaviour and not as a bribe to persuade the dog to do something you want it do: bribery may bring results in the short term but you will only make life more difficult for yourself later on.

At eight weeks old, a pup's bladder control is very weak and it needs to urinate many times a day. A puppy will usually urinate whenever it wakes throughout the day, after eating, and when excited, as well as in-between times every hour or so.

A puppy defecates 15–45 minutes after eating and the training schedule should be based around this routine. Take the pup outside on a short lead as soon as possible after it wakes, day or night. Watch it after meals and take it out when it shows signs of wanting to go to the toilet. Let it sniff around for a while and when it squats, start to praise it. When it has finished give it a treat and play with it so that it associates elimination with being outside and having fun. At other times during the day if you see it circling or if it starts whining, take it outside and go through the same routine.

litter box

If your routine means that the puppy will have to be left for longer than two hours, you will have to train it to use paper or a litter box. At this age, the pup is developing a preference for the kind of material to eliminate on. Consequently a soil tray is a much better option. Place the litter box on a large sheet of paper, and put a plastic sheet under the paper. This will help to stop the floor from smelling of urine if the pup misses the box or is late reaching it.

◁ Several thicknesses of newspaper will make a suitable indoor substrate for the pup to practice his toilet-training on.

▷ Dogs can be trained to defecate on command. If they are, then "poop-scooping" does not interfere with a good walk.

Some pups will urinate in areas that already smell of it. The puppy will still have to be trained to go outside to eliminate. It is necessary to take the puppy outside at least four times a day to associate elimination with being outside. These visits can be made in conjunction with feeding.

When you are at home at the weekend or in the evening keep a sharp eye on the puppy. If it begins to circle or whine, then take it outside as already described. A cloth should be kept handy to place under the puppy's rump when it squats to catch any leaks. If it starts to squat, startle it with a sharp shout of "No!", at the same time clapping your hands or rattling a can half-full of stones. Pick the puppy up with the cloth, take it outside and when it squats again begin to praise it. Reward it when it has finished with a treat and have a short playtime. The litter box can gradually be moved towards the door as the pup gets older and more used to using it.

puppy safety

The routine on leaving the puppy should be to confine it to a reasonably small area, preferably the place that is going to be its own area in the future. This should be entirely puppy-proof. It should not contain anything toxic that could poison the pup if chewed or swallowed, nor any article that could be chewed, swallowed and may cause an intestinal obstruction. Remove houseplants and vases of flowers. Live electrical wires should also be out of reach. The pup should have a blanket and its own bedding to rest on, suitable toys to play with, a bowl of clean drinking water and possibly a few biscuits to chew or play with. It helps to reassure the pup if the radio is left on and, if it is dark, to leave the light on as well.

△ Clicker training can be an effective means of giving the pup encouragemnt, if used regularly: one click will signal to the pup that he's done well when It is followed by a tasty reward.

▷ Perseverance and a firm training regime based on praise will result in a happy pup that is a joy to its owner.

Worming your dog

Dogs are subject to regular infestations of internal worm parasites, and treating your dog to prevent worms should be a regular part of your care routine. More frequent worming is necessary in warmer climates.

All internal parasites can cause human health problems, but the most significant risk comes from the roundworm. When a dog swallows roundworm eggs, the eggs enter the digestive system and develop into immature larvae inside the intestine. From there they migrate via the bloodstream to the lungs, are coughed up and swallowed, and travel back to the intestines where they turn into adult egg-laying worms; the cycle is then repeated. Eventually the worms' lifecycle will stimulate the canine immune system, and as a dog matures it will usually develop a resistance to roundworms.

The migration of larvae is stimulated in the bitch by pregnancy, and as the larvae can cross the placenta, newborn pups may already be infected. All puppies and dogs should be routinely treated for roundworm.

If swallowed by a human (usually a child), roundworm eggs migrate through the body in the same way as in the dog. In most cases the larvae will die in a cyst in muscle tissue,

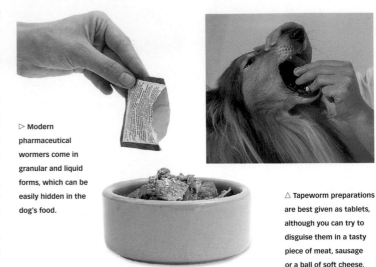

▷ **Modern pharmaceutical wormers come in granular and liquid forms, which can be easily hidden in the dog's food.**

△ **Tapeworm preparations are best given as tablets, although you can try to disguise them in a tasty piece of meat, sausage or a ball of soft cheese.**

but on rare occasions they will encyst at the back of the eyes, causing blindness. Roundworm can also weaken the human immune system, and have been associated with asthma and allergies.

Dogs can also carry several species of tapeworm, one of which can be dangerous to humans. Tapeworms have two hosts, the main one in which it is present as a worm, and an intermediate host in which it forms cysts. One particular tapeworm can exist as a worm in the dog and as a cyst in humans and other animals.

Holistic and conventional vets alike agree that alternative preparations do not provide effective control against worms. You should preventatively worm your dog three or four times a year; with worming repeated after false or real pregnancy or bouts of severe stress. Your vet can best advise on a suitable wormer for your dog. Wormer products from pet shops and supermarkets are far less effective than pharmaceutical products and need to be repeated monthly. Some of these may cause diarrhoea in the dog and are best avoided.

△ **Roundworm eggs are picked up from the soil. Tapeworm cysts are found in fleas as well as in small prey animals.**

COMPLEMENTARY TREATMENT

Alternative medicines are unlikely to give total control as wormers. Herbal preparations of *garlic* are widely used for both round- and tapeworms. *Garlic* has been shown to reduce worm numbers but has not yet been shown to be totally effective. *Wormwood* (*Artemesia absinthium*) has been used for roundworms but should not be given to pregnant bitches; *Black Walnut* has some action on tapeworms. Homeopathic remedies can control but not totally eliminate both types of worm, and are useful when physical problems associated with worms are suspected. For roundworms *Cina 30C* helps if the dog is irritable, and *Abrotanum 6C* if there is weight-loss in an otherwise fit dog. Give either twice daily for one week. For tapeworms try *Filix mas. 3X* for constipated dogs, and *Granatum 3X* if there is weight-loss. A homeopathic constitutional medicine may help control worms: see a veterinary homeopath if you wish to pursue this.

Puppy vaccinations

The diseases that we can now vaccinate dogs against used to kill many animals each year. The original vaccines were made from either dead cultures of the disease organism or from living cultures of strains that had been weakened so that when injected they stimulated the production of antibodies without causing disease. They only worked in puppies over 12 weeks old.

Now most vaccines are made using molecular engineering techniques that use only the part of the organism involved in stimulating antibody production. These can be used on pups as young as six weeks old. Some manufacturers produce multiple vaccines to be given at six, eight and ten weeks. This allows for the early socialization of the dog, which is so beneficial. They also recommend yearly boosters to make sure that the immunity is maintained.

Some breeders and owners believe that whilst modern vaccines do protect against the major diseases, they may also be involved in the increasing number of chronic diseases that are being seen. There is no alternative method of immunizing dogs against the major diseases that is recognized as safe and effective. Vaccines can be scientifically demonstrated to cause a rise in the levels of circulating antibodies (CAB) in the bloodstream, which is taken as an indication of immunity. Complementary treatments will not be considered suitable replacements for pharmaceutical vaccines until they can be proved to be effective.

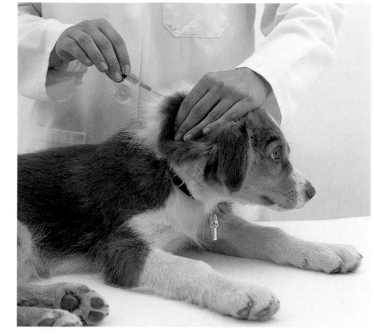

△ **Puppies should be vaccinated at 12 weeks of age. Effective modern vaccines mean that there may no longer be a need for annual re-vaccination. The re-vaccination interval is currently under review.**

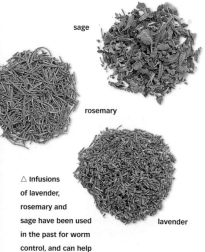

sage

rosemary

lavender

△ Infusions of lavender, rosemary and sage have been used in the past for worm control, and can help relieve the stress of first vaccinations.

COMPLEMENTARY TREATMENT

Homeopathic medicines made from the diseased tissues or discharges of infected animals (nosodes) can be used but their effectiveness has never been tested because the homeopathic community objects to infecting unprotected control animals with lethal diseases. Data from the use of nosodes is then rejected because of the lack of controlled testing. Also, there is no rise in the CAB level following nosode administration, and this is taken to indicate that nosodes are ineffective. However, George MacLeod, the pioneer of veterinary homeopathy in England, insisted there was a change in the Opsonic Index (OI) after using nosodes. The OI measures the ability of the white blood cells to destroy bacteria. A small body of work exists to support the use of nosodes in a preventative role, but if considering this as an alternative to a full vaccination programme, you are advised to have a thorough discussion with a homeopathically trained vet.

Neutering and contraception

Contraception in dogs is considered essential to prevent the birth of unwanted puppies which could become strays or may have to be put down. There are three methods of contraception for dogs. The first is to physically prevent dogs from mating, the second is chemical sterilization using tablets or injections and the third is to surgically remove the reproductive organs.

contraception

Physical prevention is not 100 per cent effective. The owner has to be on-hand when mating is about to occur to physically keep the two dogs apart. With a bitch, the owner still has the problem of twice-yearly vaginal discharges, plus the unwanted attention of male dogs to cope with.

Chemical sterilization involves giving the bitch an injection of hormones every five months, or giving a course of tablets regularly before she is expected to come on heat. The disadvantage of sterilization is that it may increase the chance of the bitch developing serious uterine problems in later life, although the manufacturers claim that the risk is small. The treatment is not permanent, however, and if the medication is stopped, the bitch can breed. In these circumstances it is best to let the bitch have one cycle and mate her at the following cycle. This method can also be used as a temporary method of preventing the bitch from coming on heat at an inconvenient time – such as if there a new baby or serious illness in the family.

neutering

The method of choice for most animal welfare organizations is removal of the dog's reproductive organs. For bitches this is spaying, where an ovario-hysterectomy is performed, an operation to remove the ovaries and uterus. Spaying ensures that a bitch can never have puppies. Although no surgery is 100 per cent safe, the risks from surgery and anaesthetic are now much reduced. Spaying has the advantage of stopping unwanted discharges, preventing the development of uterine troubles and, if performed before the first season, of reducing the chances of mammary tumours later on in life. However, the operation is irreversible.

The age at which spaying should be done is controversial. Rescue societies suggest as young as 12 weeks to ensure that the dog's new owner can never breed from her. Some vets suggest operating just before the first heat, at five months, because the procedure is easier than in a mature bitch and it still reduces the likelihood of mammary tumours developing in later life. Others prefer to operate between the first and second heat. The bitch will then have gone through a full cycle of hormone changes and is fully developed, both physiologically and emotionally. Some vets believe that bitches operated on after the first heat have a smaller chance of becoming uncontrollably obese and of developing incontinence in later life.

For male dogs castration is strongly recommended by animal welfare societies. Apart from helping towards birth control, it can have an effect on the dog's behaviour. Castration is often recommended in cases of aggression. However, aggression is more often due to poor training and socializing than to excessive hormone levels, and castration only seems to have an effect in

CASTRATION

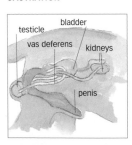

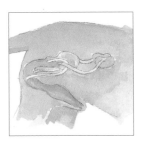

entire dog

castrated dog

SPAYING

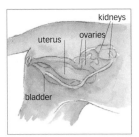

entire bitch

spayed bitch

△ Castration involves the complete removal of both testicles. They are usually removed through a small incision just in front of the pelvis and not through the scrotum itself because the dog's scrotum bleeds more heavily after being cut than most other species. Cutting or ligating the vas deferens does result in sterility, but male hormones are still produced by the testes, and the dog's libido and behaviour will remain unchanged.

△ A total ovario-hysterectomy is the preferred method of neutering a female dog. Although the bitch would be made sterile by a hysterectomy or by ligating the fallopian tubes, female hormones would still be produced by the ovaries. The presence of these hormones would mean that she would still cycle and attract dogs, and her desire to mate could be inconvenient for the owner.

about 50 per cent of behavioural cases. Castration is more successful in cases associated with prostate problems, such as hyper-sexuality, tumours and enlarged prostate. There is an anti-male hormone which can be tried before castration. If the injection improves the dog's behaviour, it increases the chance that castration will be effective, although this is not a 100 per cent guarantee. Finally, there are some cases of epilepsy that do respond well to hormone treatment and in such cases castration is definitely worth trying.

The biggest difficulty faced by many dog owners on the issues of neutering and contraception is ethical. Do we have the moral right to neuter an animal, particularly when our main reason for doing so is to avoid cost and inconvenience to ourselves? Reproduction is an essential part of life. It has been claimed that it is the prime reason for living. The hormone system is a major body system, and interfering with it can have a major effect on the body and mind – as is sometimes seen in women following a hysterectomy and in men who have had a vasectomy. It is a delicate issue and there are no easy answers.

◁ High levels of male hormones can be responsible for some forms of aggression. In such cases, hormonal treatment can be tried before deciding on castration.

▽ A massage with essential oil of sage, diluted in a carrier oil, may be beneficial to the bitch after spaying because of its action as a vulnerary and its association with the female tract.

sage

Reproduction in a healthy bitch

Regardless of the species, reproduction is an animal's most important function. However, breeding from a domestic dog requires a serious amount of commitment from the owner, and before you can decide whether or not to breed from your dog, you should be aware of what is involved.

Bitches become sexually mature between 5–15 months, usually at 6–8 months. Every six months, a healthy bitch will have a three-week cycle of hormone changes, during which her vulva swells, discharges start, she attracts dogs and she ovulates. Ovulation takes place around the 10th–11th day of her cycle. This is when she is most likely to be mated successfully.

If a bitch is mated but does not become pregnant, she may have a false pregnancy. This means she will go through the nesting procedure and produce milk even though she is not carrying puppies. In the wild, she would adopt the role of foster mother for orphaned or abandoned pups. While a domesticated bitch is nesting, changes may occur in her personality which are disturbing to her owners. She may become surly and not want to exercise, or she may mother her toys and become excessively possessive about them. Complementary treatments are available to help restore balance to a bitch with a false pregnancy, however (see *The Female System*).

should I breed from my dog?

Today, the majority of bitches are spayed and breeding is concentrated in the hands of a small group of professionals whose aim is to keep the breed pure. The vast majority of breeders take a pride in the health and well-being of their stock, and derive great pleasure in exhibiting them at shows. There are unfortunately a few maverick puppy farmers who are more interested in financial profit than the good of the breed.

One of the most common reasons for mating a pet bitch is when the owner plans to spay her but feels that the bitch would benefit from the experience of motherhood before being spayed. However, probably as many bitches react with resentment after spaying once they have had pups as bitches who have not had a litter. It doesn't seem to make much difference.

Breeding is much more expensive than most people realize. If you let nature take its course, the resultant mongrels will be difficult to home. If you have a controlled mating you will have to pay a stud fee to the male dog's owners. The bitch will need extra food in the last third of pregnancy and while she is feeding the puppies, and the pups need feeding until they are homed. You will need to provide a whelping-box for the birth and first few weeks, and a suitable exercise area for the pups after that. The bitch will need worming before and after whelping, and the pups will need to be wormed three times after they have been weaned. A still birth or Caesarean section may incur additional vet's fees. Breeding is unlikely to be profitable unless it also accompanies success in the showring or is done as a business. The former is a serious commitment and the latter is immoral.

△ **A low potency dose of homeopathic arnica can help lift the feeling of physical exhaustion that can accompany pregnancy.**

If you decide to breed from a pet bitch, talk it over with your vet and the breeder from whom you bought her. Some breeds have more inherited faults than others, and some – especially those with large heads and small pelvises – are often incapable of whelping naturally. Your vet can advise you as to inherited faults, any pre-mating tests or X-rays that should be done and the risks of pregnancy in general. Ethical questions are involved when a breed is certain to need a Caesarean section, or is subject to a high risk of inherited disease.

pregnancy and birth

Bitches whelp 61–66 days after mating. Let your vet know when your bitch has been mated: a manual pregnancy test, which is 90 per cent effective, can be performed between the 22nd and 28th days. Blood tests and ultra-sonic scans can be done from the 35th day and are more accurate. A pregnant bitch can be helped if given an infusion of *Raspberry Leaf* tea daily throughout the pregnancy, or homeopathic *Caulophyllum 30C* weekly for the last three weeks.

the birthing

When she begins to have the pups the bitch will lie on her side and there will be some movement of the abdominal wall. At this point let the vet know she is starting. When the birth begins she will squat down on her haunches and push very hard. At this stage, give *Caulophyllum* every 15 minutes to help the uterus contract and the cervix to open. If she has been pushing hard for half an hour, or if there has been a big fluid discharge, or if part of the membranes, or a pup, have been seen and she has not yet delivered, seek veterinary help. The interval between pups can vary from ten minutes to several hours. If there has been an interval of two hours and the bitch is still resting, let the vet know. He may not want to do anything immediately but he can prepare to help when needed.

the delivery

When the bitch delivers a pup she should break the membranes and begin to clean it. She can be allowed to eat two or three of the membranes, because they contain hormones which will help her to continue with the whelping. Her licking the pup with her rough tongue helps to stimulate its breathing. If she does not know what to do, or has the pups more quickly than she can cope with, break the membranes and give the pup a good rub with a dry coarse towel. This helps to dry the pup and will prevent chilling. Rubbing around the pup's nose, umbilicus and anus will simulate the mother's actions and help the pup to breathe. There is no rush to break the umbilical cord. At the moment of birth the pup's blood is evenly distributed between the body and the membranes.

◁ Bach Flowers, such as walnut and mustard, can help lift post-natal gloom.

You can give the membranes two or three minutes to contract and push all the blood into the body. The cord can then be broken or cut about 2.5cm (1in) from the body, after first tying it with a piece of boiled cotton thread.

If you notice that a pup cannot or is reluctant to breathe, clear as much mucus as possible out of the throat using your little finger. If the nose and chest seem full of mucus, you can help by holding the pup in your cupped hands, head downwards, and supporting the head and neck. Then, swing your hands and the pup vertically downwards, stopping abruptly at the bottom of the swing. Inertia and gravity working together on the mucus should help it to come out. Respiration can also be stimulated by giving one or two drops of the Bach Flower *Rescue Remedy* directly into the pup's mouth, or two drops of a solution of a homeopathic *Carbo veg.* tablet dissolved in 10ml (2tsp) of water. The airways must be clear if either of these medicines are to work. If the pup's breathing is rattling because of fluid in the chest, homeopathic *Antimony tart.* given in the same way as the *Carbo veg.* is helpful.

△ Looking after a large litter can be as demanding for the owner as it is for the mother. Patience is needed by both parties until the pups are old enough to leave the dam.

aftercare

After the whelping has ended, a dose of homeopathic *Arnica 30C* can be given to the bitch every two hours for three doses particularly if it was a difficult birth, and a liquid preparation of *Arnica* can be given to the pups. Homeopathic *Sepia 30C* can be given twice daily for up to three days following whelping, to shrink the uterus and expel any remaining membranes.

raspberry leaf

△ Raspberry leaf infusions are the traditional herbal tonic for the female tract.

Holistic Dog Care

Many times an illness begins when one is unaware of an imbalance that has

subtly begun. Do not forget that the myriad things of the universe have an

intimate relationship with one another.

The Yellow Emperor's Classic of Medicine, 250BC

Holistic therapies

The basic philosophy underlying holistic medicine is a concern for the living totality of the patient. Its aim is to treat the patient as a whole and not the disease in isolation.

Holistic treatment is not aimed at the cause of the infection or the suppression of symptoms but at all aspects of the patient's life, including the patient's mental and emotional state, any co-existing physical complaints, lifestyle, stresses and nutritional status. While Western medicine looks for the true name of the disease (the diagnosis), and for the correct treatment to cure the patient, holistic medicine looks at a much wider concept of disease. It recognizes that a range of treatments may be necessary, from simple lifestyle changes to surgery and conventional medicines, and accepts that therapies which cannot be explained by science can affect the whole organism, and are often essential if a true cure is to be achieved.

In human medicine, there are holistic clinics where patients are treated by teams of therapists under the supervision of a doctor. The patient's response to treatment is closely monitored and the treatment is varied accordingly. In the veterinary field, things are not so sophisticated. There is a growing number of veterinary practices worldwide offering alternative and complementary healthcare advice but the range of services available in many areas is still very limited.

There are also legal restraints in holistic practice for animals. The law recognizes that humans understand the risks involved in seeking non-medically qualified treatment. Because an animal is incapable of assessing risk, the treatment of disease in animals is restricted to veterinary surgeons only. Vets are allowed to work with the help of qualified physiotherapists, osteopaths and chiropractors, but the more esoteric therapies can only be carried out by the dog's owner or by vets who are suitably qualified – and of these there are very few.

Of the complementary therapies offered by vets, homeopathy and acupuncture are the most common. These are complete systems of medicine, each with their own philosophy of health and disease. Both see disease as an imbalance of energy in the organism. Homeopathy recognizes the presence in the body of a "Vital Force" which attempts to keep the body in a state of good health. Disease is seen as a disturbance of that force and symptoms as the body's attempt to regain equilibrium. The symptoms are then used to find the curative medicine. Homeopathy also believes that lifestyle circumstances may predispose us to disease and that these must be eliminated if a cure is to result.

Acupuncture is a branch of Traditional Chinese Medicine. This system sees energy as flowing round the physical body along invisible channels known as "meridians". Disease occurs when this energy flow is disturbed. Stimulation of specific points on the meridians restores balance to the system and health to the body.

Ayurvedic medicine is an Indian holistic system with its own philosophy of disease. It recognizes a flow of energy, which it calls "prana", through channels known as "nadis". The major nadis have energy vortices or "chakras". Treatment is based on herbal medicine and diet. It is less common in the Western world than acupuncture and homeopathy.

Therapies which work at the energy level include Bach Flower remedies and crystal therapy. Bach Flower remedies are chosen purely on the emotional state of the patient. Crystal therapy attempts to use the energy given off by crystals to restore balance to the energy field of the body.

Widely practised holisitic therapies include herbalism, aromatherapy, massage, osteopathy, chiropractic and physiotherapy. Therapies such as these with a physical basis are more generally accepted by vets.

If you wish to use holistic therapies on your dog, discuss the matter first with a vet in order to make sure that any essential conventional medical care is given before a complementary treatment plan is worked out between you.

◁ **Good dog health is a question of mental, emotional and physical balance; food and water alone can only ensure survival.**

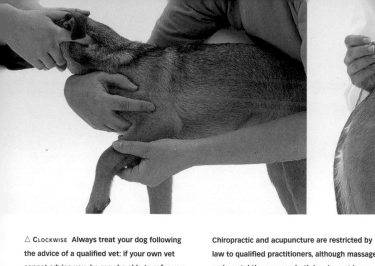

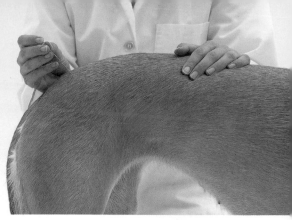

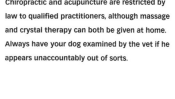

△ CLOCKWISE Always treat your dog following the advice of a qualified vet: if your own vet cannot advise you, he may be able to refer you to a colleague or an organization which deals more specifically in holistic veterinary care.

Chiropractic and acupuncture are restricted by law to qualified practitioners, although massage and crystal therapy can both be given at home. Always have your dog examined by the vet if he appears unaccountably out of sorts.

Physical therapies: massage

Massage is the oldest and simplest physical therapy. Its most basic but profound form is when the mother "rubs it better" for her child. The fact that the skin and nervous system develop from the same cell layer when in embroyo may have something to do with the reason that massage calms the mind as well as the body, and gives a sense of complete well-being.

Giving your dog a massage will induce a feeling of well-being in the dog, and can help to establish a valuable non-verbal communication that conveys an attitude of loving care. This strengthens the bond between dog and owner, and the sense of harmony that this generates will help to heal not only the dog's physical body but its mind and spirit as well. The act of giving a massage is therapeutic for the owner and has been found to reduce stress levels.

Physically, massage improves the dog's circulation, relaxes the muscles and helps to balance muscle function and joint action, and can help to disperse scar tissue. It also helps the lymphatic system to speed-up the

rate at which it detoxifies the body. It may also increase the production of the body's natural pain killers (endorphins) which help to increase the feeling of well-being.

Massage can be used as an aid to keeping a healthy dog fit. It should not be used to treat sick animals unless they have first been checked by a vet. It should definitely not be used in cases where there is severe pain or the skin is damaged or infected. Nor where there is muscle injury, or where there are severe joint pains. Massage is also contra-indicated where the dog has recently had a high temperature (in the case of an acute infection for example), and when the dog is known to have high blood pressure. The latter is difficult to recognize as techniques for measuring the blood pressure of dogs are still being developed.

massage routine

A simple routine for an owner would be to begin with a few gentle strokes of even pressure along the body and limbs in the direction of the hair growth. These strokes

should be slow and rhythmic and will help to relax the dog. They also allow the owner to locate any tender spots. Lubricants are not normally required, but if they are, baby powder is preferred to the oils used on humans; these make the fingers slide too quickly over the skin for the massage to be effective, and they can get very messy.

The pressure of the strokes should be gradually increased to a firmness that the dog will tolerate. Change the direction of the strokes to work towards the heart so as to stimulate venous and lymphatic drainage. Ideally one would start at the feet and move upwards and forwards towards the head. If, however, the dog is footshy it may be better to start at the head and work back along the body.

The dog's feet should be massaged slowly and gently with the fingers, getting into the spaces between the toes if possible. Massage the legs upwards towards the body, starting just above the paw. Use your fingers for small dogs and your palm where possible for larger dogs.

DIAGNOSTIC MASSAGE POINTS IN A DOG

Pressure on these points can elicit a pain response to indicate potential problem areas:

a – ear
b – teeth and gums
c – throat and neck
d – back and spine
e – anal glands
f – hips
g – bladder
h – abdomen
i – lower abdomen and liver
j – ribs and lungs
k – ribs and lungs
l – elbow
m – shoulder
n – feet and toes
o – hoch (ankle)
p – stifle (knee)
x – kidney and ovary

Massage

Most dogs love the attention of a massage and are quite happy to stand still while you pummel them gently from head to toe. You will find the experience almost as therapeutic for yourself. A regular massage will certainly improve your relationship with your dog. Add a simple massage at the end of your daily grooming routine.

◁ **1** When first using massage on your dog, or if your dog is known to be footshy, start off with his head. Place your hands on his head and, with light pressure, start with slow strokes, moving down over the ears. Repeat several times until you feel your dog relax. Extend the strokes over the head, around the eyes, nose, mouth and ears.

△ **2** Move slowly down the neck to the back area. Keep your hands on either side of the spine (*never* massage directly on the spine) and make long rhythmic stokes in the direction of the heart.

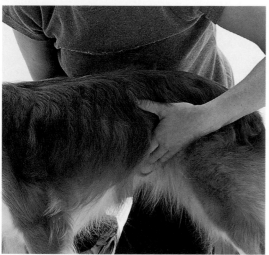

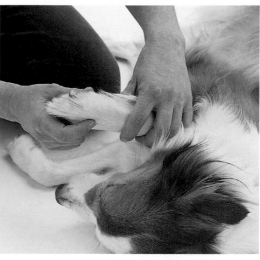

△ **3** Slide your hands round the dog's sides to the abdomen and make circular movements over the belly and groin area, using your fingers or the palms of your hands, depending on the size of the dog.

△ **4** Massage the shoulder and chest, then move down each leg towards the foot. The feet should be massaged very slowly and gently: try and rub between the toes if the dog will let you.

To tackle the abdomen, either keep the dog standing or get him to roll over. Massage with circular movements, again using either your palms or fingers depending on the size of the dog. The body and chest are best massaged first on one side and then the other. Start at the rear of the body and work towards the dog's head.

The spine should *never* be massaged. Instead, massage slightly to each side of the midline using the finger tips. It is here that you are most likely to find the tender trigger points. Do not massage these points at all vigorously. It will cause the surrounding muscles to go into spasm as a protective reflex. Light massage will help to reduce the reactivity of the point and to induce relaxation of the muscles. Finger pressure on a trigger point can deactivate it, whilst vigorous massage can increase the pain by stimulating further muscle contractions in an attempt to protect the damaged area.

Finally move to the head and neck. This stage of the massage is a favourite with most dogs, and you may like to give a few minutes extra attention here. Massage the head area gently, including around the eyes, nose, mouth and ears, remembering to stroke and not to poke. The neck should be treated as an elongation of the back, and massage applied to the side and not to the middle. End the session with a few light strokes along the body from head to tail.

Physical therapies: physiotherapy

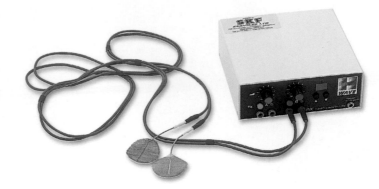

This therapy supplements the medical and surgical treatment of any condition that has a major impact on the musculoskeletal, or locomotor, system and the circulation. It includes everything from the simplest massage to the use of complex apparatus to stimulate muscle tissue. It is part of mainstream conventional medicine, yet is also a vital component of holistic medicine. Good physiotherapy can help to control pain, speed-up healing and preserve the function of injured tissue. It can be used alongside surgery, pharmaceutical medicines and all complementary therapies.

Training in animal physiotherapy usually begins with a course in human anatomy and physiology. Qualified physiotherapists are state-registered and are legally recognized. They are not allowed to diagnose the condition from which a patient is suffering (that is the province of the doctor) but once a medical diagnosis has been made, they are allowed to treat the patient under the doctor's supervision. In order to practise on animals, some physiotherapists undertake additional veterinary training. If you or your vet think that physiotherapy would help your dog, you are advised to enlist the help of a veterinary physiotherapist, if at all possible: not only will a qualified animal physiotherapist be more familiar with the dog's anatomy, they also will be more able to handle the animal.

Veterinary physiotherapy is commonly performed on professional sport animals such as racehorses and Greyhounds, and is slowly becoming more widely used in general small animal veterinary practices. The objective of physiotherapy is to regain the strength and full range of movement, and this can be achieved either by manual manipulation or by a series of controlled exercises. The exercises are made more comfortable for the damaged animal by the use of treatments such as cold and heat, electrical stimulation and laser therapy.

Therapeutic use of cold is applied as quickly as possible after an injury in the form of a cold compress to reduce the seepage of blood and other fluids into surrounding tissue. It also decreases muscle spasms and reduces nerve pain. A plastic beaker filled with water and frozen can be used as a cold compress on large areas and surgical wounds two to four times a day, for up to 20 minutes at a time.

Therapeutic warmth is used 72 hours after an injury to increase blood circulation in the damaged tissue. This helps to remove waste products and increases nourishment of the area, speeding up healing, relieving tension and reducing pain.

△ The H Wave machine passes warm currents of heat to the injured area to energize the tissue and encourage relaxtion. As the muscle tissue starts to relax, the tension is released.

Electrical stimulation has a variety of benefits. Special equipment can be used to help with pain relief and to stimulate muscle contractions. The latter can help to counteract muscle wastage, reduce spasm pains and increase muscle strength. It can also increase blood flow in damaged tissue and where there are certain forms of circulatory disease. This also aids healing.

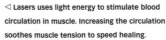

◁ Lasers uses light energy to stimulate blood circulation in muscle. Increasing the circulation soothes muscle tension to speed healing.

△ Palpation of the neck area. The hands feel the muscles for tightness, which indicates tension. The dog's response to the contact pressure may indicate painful areas.

△ Palpation of the mid-spinal area. The hands are placed at the sides of the spine to check for pain, muscle spasm, tension or heat swelling. The hand hold mobilizes the tight, painful soft tissues in order to release constriction and improve the circulation.

△ Placing the pads of the H Wave machine over the soft spinal tissue will stimulate the muscles in the same way as the hand hold. Heat from the machine will relax the muscle tissue, freeing the muscles from tension and reducing pain.

Ultrasound is used to provide a form of heat therapy by using the energy of ultra-sonic vibrations to warm the tissues beneath the skin, which helps to increase the amount by which scar and other fibrous tissue can stretch. This allows the remodelling of scar tissue and helps to reduce the amount of scar tissue that does form. It can also help to deactivate painful muscular trigger points when properly used by trained operatives. Ultrasound treatment must never be used after exercise: it can have the opposite effect of increasing pain by overheating the tissue, causing further damage.

Exercise can be used in physiotherapy to increase strength, endurance and flexibility. Dogs recuperating from injuries are often given stretching exercises, and these can be very useful; the physiotherapist's will perform the manually assisted stretches after the dog has been warmed-up by light exercise. Repeated, gentle stretching will help to reduce muscle spasms and promote elongation of tissue, giving a greater range of movement.

Manual stretching must never overstretch the damaged tissues, or be done without the dog being warmed up first, or if there is an acute inflammation. If there is acute pain, ice-packs should be applied. Hydrotherapy,

or swimming in warm water, can help convalescing dogs to stretch their limbs safely without manual assistance. Exercise with weights and other equipment used in human physiotherapy is not easily adapted to canine therapy. However, under the right circumstances, malleable lead weights can be attached to the dog's limbs to give extra resistance to its movements.

Simple massage and the use of ice-packs and gentle warmth may be tried by owners as self-help treatments at home. However, more specialist physiotherapy techniques can inflict further injury if misapplied, and these should only be used by a qualified physiotherapist; a physiotherapist without a veterinary qualification should always work under the guidance of a vet.

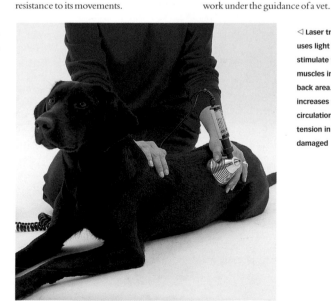

◁ Laser treatment uses light energy to stimulate the soft muscles in the lower back area. The laser increases the blood circulation to release tension in the damaged area.

Physical therapies: osteopathy

This is a form of treatment based on the manipulation of the body's bony skeleton. Osteopathy is not a complete system of medicine. The basic premise is that disease results from the changes that occur in all parts of the body when one part of its structure is altered.

The founder of osteopathy, an American, Dr Andrew Taylor Still, saw the skeleton as having a dual purpose. The commonly recognized function was that it provided the physical framework for the body. By the action of the muscles that were attached to it, it allowed the mechanical movement of the body. Its other, and equally important function was to protect the vital organs of the body. Dr Still theorized that if the skeleton were out of alignment, the body it supported and protected would not be able to maintain a state of good health. The fundamental basis of all osteopathy is that structure governs function.

Osteopathy is now recognized as a valid treatment that is complementary to and supportive of orthodox Western medicine. Osteopaths are trained to treat each patient as a complete structure, paying particular attention to the relationship between the musculoskeletal system and the function of the body. They are taught how to assess a patient's medical history, and how to examine the patient. From the patient's history they will decide if osteopathy is a suitable treatment. A physical examination enables them to observe the ease and range of movement that the patient has in the limbs and spine. By carefully feeling the muscles and bones, the osteopath can locate painful areas and identify any misalignments of the skeleton. The osteopath is then able to make a diagnosis of the problem and develop a treatment plan.

Osteopathic treatment for dogs uses soft-tissue massage techniques and joint manipulation to make adjustments to the damaged neuro-musculoskeletal structure. The techniques on dogs used are similar to those used on humans. Manipulation techniques make corrections which repair the damage and allow healing to occur. Having given the first treatment, the osteopath will monitor improvements by sight and by feeling the changes that occur in the diseased area and in the dog's body in general.

The massage element of osteopathy is designed to increase blood flow and thereby increase the rate of elimination of toxic waste products that build up in damaged areas. It also increases the oxygenation of the tissues, and this will help to relieve pain and stiffness.

The most common joint-manipulation technique used on osteopathy is the high velocity thrust. Contrary to popular belief, although this causes popping or cracking noises, it does not realign bones and joints. It does, however, slightly separate the joint surfaces momentarily. This separation of the bone surfaces stretches the joint capsule and this permits the joint to move more freely over a wider range of angles. At the time that the joint capsule is stretched, tiny bubbles of carbon dioxide come out of solution and this is responsible for the audible popping sound.

The other techniques used in osteopathy are passive movement and articulation. Both of these techniques are designed to stretch the soft-tissues gently and painlessly to result in greater joint and limb mobility. Passive movement involves the osteopath gently moving the dog's limbs while the dog relaxes and makes no physical effort. Articulation takes this one stage further. It involves using the dog's limbs as levers by which to stretch the soft tissue. In all three techniques, the osteopath monitors the dog's response and makes adjustments to the treatment plan accordingly.

Osteopathy is officially recognized as a valid therapy for animals, although there are as yet no recognized schools of veterinary osteopathy. If you wish to have your dog treated osteopathically, it must have been examined initially by a vet. If the vet thinks the treatment would be beneficial, a qualified human osteopath will carry out treatment under the vet's direction. It is important that the vet and the osteopath cooperate with each other. The vet's notes, diagnosis and treatment schedule should be made available to the osteopath, and the osteopath should liaise about the proposed treatment, potential benefits and eventual outcome. Failure to liaise effectively can result in inappropriate treatment being given, and this may have an adverse effect on the dog. Many osteopaths use other therapies in support of their treatment of human patients, such as aromatherapy essential oils. However, by law they are not allowed to use techniques other than osteopathy on dogs without the permission of the vet.

It must be remembered that while the theory of osteopathy is valid for all species, its application in dogs is made more difficult because patient feedback is an impossibility and cooperation cannot be guaranteed from one session to the next. When the dog does cooperate, however, good results can be achieved.

WHEN TO USE OSTEOPATHY

In the absence of scientific research it is difficult to evaluate the value of osteopathy on dogs. However, where vets have referred individual cases to human osteopaths, the results have been encouraging. Osteopathy appears particularly useful as a form of pain control for joint discomfort resulting from road traffic accidents, sports injuries and degenerative diseases.

If the dog refuses to cooperate once treatment begins, do not force it. You can either defer the session to a later date, or consider another therapy after discussing the options with your vet.

General osteopathic treatment

The initial stage of any osteopathic treatment is a total examination of the dog. The osteopath works through a sequence of movements to manipulate the dog's limbs so as to identify a suspected misalignment. Note the gentleness of the techniques: this dog did not even need to be held.

△ **2** Examination and articulation of the hip, stifle and hoch. Each back leg is extended to stretch the muscles in the front of the thigh.

△ **1** Examination and articulation of the shoulder. Each front legs is extended to stretch the muscles.

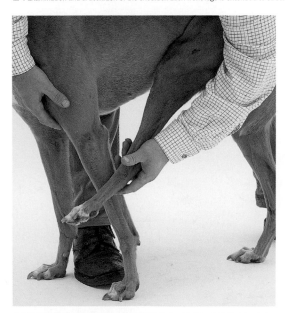

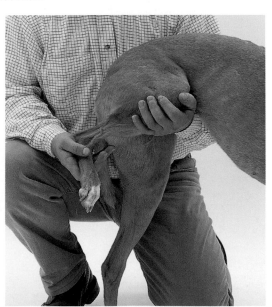

△ **3** Examination and articulation of the hip in flexion. Each back leg is extended to stretch the hamstring muscles.

△ **4** Examination and articulation of the hip in abduction, and of the pelvis and lumbar spine in rotation.

Physical therapies: chiropractic

Like osteopathy, chiropractic concentrates on the anatomy and physiology of the dog's musculoskeletal and nervous systems, and on the safe manipulation of the spine. The difference between the two therapies lies in their basic philosophy of disease.

Chiropractic theory says that if vertebral segments of the spine are malaligned, there will be undue pressure on the spinal cord or spinal nerves. This can cause interference with nerve transmissions, which may result in abnormal function and disease. If the malfunctioning vertebral segment can be repositioned by manipulation, the abnormal pressures on the spinal nerve roots are relieved and normal nerve function is restored to the affected area, including the tissues controlled by that segment.

The first stage of chiropractic treatment with a human patient involves taking a detailed case history, and an examination of the nerves (nerologicial examination) and bones (orthopaedic examination). These same tests are carried out on a dog. The neurological examination includes reflex and nerve stretch testing; the orthopaedic examination tests the range of movement of the various regions of the spine. At the same time positions that cause pain are noted, as are any abnormal movement of the joints of the spine. Chiropractors are also trained to take X-rays (radiography). Radiography is used to rule out the existence of any spinal disease that might cause a similar clinical condition, and to rule out the possibility of serious spinal damage, such as fractures after recent accidents.

The chiropractor is concerned with the physical effect created by any restriction of movement of the spine, however small and subtle this may appear. A change in align-ment of the surfaces of the small vertebral joints, together with the associated nerve dysfunction, is known as a subluxation, a term used by vets to describe partial dislocations. Chiropractic diagnosis aims to recognize such restrictions and gives

treatment to adjust them. The adjustment seldom results in total correction but initiates the body's natural healing processes, which slowly complete the realignment. Chiropractic adjustment is carried out by carefully applying a high-velocity short-amplitude thrust to the appropriate small facet joints of the vertebrae. Properly performed, an adjustment will correct the mechanical function of the joint and restore normal nerve function in the area.

As with osteopathy, this realignment of the joints is accomplished by a stretching of the joint capsule, and the same popping noise occurs due to the release of carbon dioxide within the joint. In severe or long-standing cases, treatment is often given in a series of adjustments designed to give a gradual return to normal function rather than in one or two more traumatic ones. Chiropractors are also taught deep-tissue massage techniques. These are used to support their manipulations, particularly in chronic cases. Drugs are never used in chiropractic treatment.

Few colleges of chiropractic include veterinary training in the syllabus. The one veterinary chiropractic college in the UK is the McTimoney College of Chiropractic, while in the United States, the American Veterinary Chiropractic Association runs courses for vets and human chiropractors.

As with osteopathy, the treatment of dogs (and other animals) by chiropractic is permitted by law, provided that treatment is given under the supervision of a vet. Either a human chiropractor or an animal-trained one is allowed by law to treat a dog, but if you are given the choice, remember that the animal practitioner's training will have involved animal handling, and there is more chance that he will persuade the dog to cooperate.

If you are having your dog treated by a chiropractor, try to encourage a good level of communication between the practitioner and the vet. The vet may be required to take any X-rays needed by the chiropractor for the efficient treatment of the dog, but a full examination may not be possible because of the animal's dislike of it. Treatment can be equally difficult to give.

In spite of the difficulties involved with treating dogs, chiropractic does have a place in modern holistic treatment of dogs who suffer the equivalent of back pain and spinal injuries. Because drugs are not involved, the treatment is entirely non-toxic. Adverse effects can sometimes occur after treatment, although these cases are rare. As with any therapy, however, it is worth discussing the possibility of things getting worse before they get better with both the vet and the chiropractor before starting treatment.

WHEN TO USE CHIROPRACTIC

Chiropractic is not for home use. Because treatment involves manipulation of the spine, the consequences of misapplied techniques can be severe and could lead to the dog suffering paralysis. Even after observing the actions of a trained chiropractor during treatment sessions with your dog, never attempt to treat your dog yourself.

If you are having your dog treated, pay attention to its instinctive response to the practitioner. On subsequent visits to the clinic in particular, watch for signs of reluctance, the need to escape, or defensive aggression. This may be your dog's way of telling you that he dislikes the treatment, and no matter how beneficial you and your vet and/or chiropractor have decided the treatment can be for your dog, if the dog does not feel comfortable with the treatment, you need to put an end to the sessions and reassess the alternatives. A resentful dog cannot be treated successfully.

McTimoney chiropractic

The following sequence shows the checking procedure that is done before the problem can be diagnosed and treatment given. All types of ailments are treated by McTimoney Chiropractic, from strains and lameness to the animal's inability to move normally, for example, jumping out of the car or over a hurdle. Treatments can be given weekly or monthly until the problem has cleared. In general, six-monthly check-ups are advised after a course of treatment has been completed.

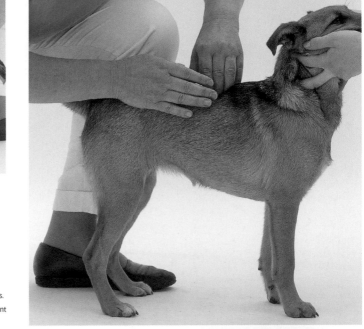

△ **1** The following movements make up the chiropractic checking procedure for all animals. If a subluxation is located, the movements are adjusted accordingly. Here, both hands are placed behind the dog's neck as the practitioner first checks the Atlas, which lies at the base of the ears.

▷ **2** The next stage is to check the spine for subluxations. Here, the McTimoney practitioner is making an adjustment of the thoracic spine.

△ **3** The practitioner positions the hind legs to check for subluxations in the pelvis area and the stifle (knee) joint.

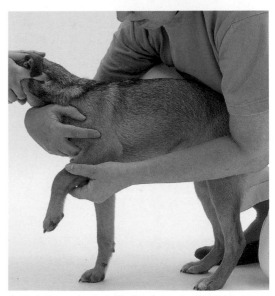

△ **4** The forelegs are then checked for signs of subluxations in the joints and elbow, which could be causing lameness.

Physical therapies: T touch

This is a form of manipulation that differs from massage in that it affects the skin only and not the underlying tissues. Rhythmic, gentle finger touches are applied to the dog's body to calm and relax it and to improve its capacity for training. T Touch therapy is particularly useful for frightened dogs.

The idea for the therapy was developed by Linda Tellington-Jones, a Canadian physiotherapist who worked with horses before extending the techniques to all other animals, including dogs. Tellington-Jones developed the therapy from the work of Dr Moshe Feldenkrais, an Israeli writer who was at the time teaching physical body awareness to humans. The theory is that non-habitual movements combined with gentle manipulations can promote body awareness, and that this in turn can affect behaviour. The system behind the therapy is known as the Tellington-Jones Every Animal Method (TTEAM), and the individual strokes are known as T Touch.

The basic principle behind the T Touch strokes is that the skin is moved in a circular motion through just over 360 degrees. If you imagine a clockface on the surface of the skin, the movement works clockwise from 6 o'clock, through 12 o'clock and continues to the 8 o'clock position. Studies have shown that one effect of the technique is to change brain activity. Changes are seen in the *alpha*, *beta*, *delta* and *theta* waves of horses and the people who administer the therapy. It has the effect of stimulating the nervous system and benefiting both the mental and emotional spheres.

Skin manipulation is done with two or three fingers depending on the size of the dog; the thumb and heel of the hand rest on the body while the relaxed fingers move the skin. Only one circle is made in any one position; the hand is then slid to an adjacent area of skin and another circle made, with the sliding action connecting the circles. Whilst one hand makes the circles, the other hand rests on the skin close to the working hand to complete the connection between owner and dog (it also helps the owner to balance as they perform the strokes).

There are fifteen T Touch movements, each one using different parts of the fingers and hand, different pressures and different speeds of movement. The techniques used include back and belly lifts, crossways movements across the belly, manipulation of the ears from base to tip (to stimulate the acupuncture points in the ear) and, if the dog will allow it, circles made in and around the mouth, lips and nose.

Dogs that resent being handled are often better if held on a halter rather than a collar and lead, with the circles made with the end of a soft flexible wand or feather.

The main benefit of T Touch is that it helps to increase the bond between dog and owner, and relaxes the animal when it is frightened and stressed. It can also be useful during recovery from accidents and surgery.

△ The Clouded Leopard is suitable for delicate areas such as the head. The secret here is for light pressure and a nimble hand movement.

△ As its name suggests, the Tarantula Pulling the Plow moves in a spidery pathway across larger areas of the body such as the neck and shoulders.

1 the clouded leopard

2 the lying leopard

3 the racoon

4 the snail's pace

5 the bear

6 feathering

7 the abalone

8 the lick of the cow's tongue

9 the tiger t touch

10 Noah's march

11 the python lift

12 the butterfly

13 tarantulas pulling the plow

14 belly lifts

15 back lifts

The Leopard The Clouded Leopard is so called because of the light and stealthy hand contact; while the Lying Leopard uses a firmer pressure and a flatter hand position to give a more defined contact. The Leopard movements are used to focus an excited dog.

The Racoon Use for smaller dogs and delicate work; for working around wounds; to speed healing; to increase circulation and activate neural impulses in the lower legs; to reduce swelling without causing pain.

The Snail's Pace The slow contractions and extensions of the fingers are used to relax back and neck muscles, to improve breathing and to reduce stress.

The Bear For areas of heavy muscling, such as the shoulders, back and flank. The emphasis is on the fingernails making the contact, rather than the finger pads. The circle is made with the fingers pointing down, parting layers of muscle rather than digging into them.

Feathering For dogs who are frightened of being touched, in place of the Bear. The movement should be light and fast.

The Abalone This mimics the slow, circular motion of the sea abalone. It is not so much a movement as a firm, calming pressure that pushes the skin around the circle.

The Lick of the Cow's Tongue A gentle, swiping movement upwards from the belly to the back to soothe and calm a nervous or anxious dog. On very sensitive animals, the skin may twitch. If this happens, stop the movement and make a light Abalone circle before moving on to the next area. This encourages calm breathing, and will discourage the dog from pulling away on contact.

The Tiger Touch A movement for heavily muscled dogs, and for itch relief. The fingernails are the point of contact, and because the fingers are raised and apart, the nails almost seem to make their own individual circles.

Noah's Ark Use these long, firm strokes to close a TTouch session: after the experience of revivification that the TTouch has brought to individual parts of the body, Noah's Ark will bring back a sense of wholeness. Using both hands, begin at the dog's head and make long, smooth strokes over the entire body.

The Python Lift Use on the shoulders, legs, neck and chest areas to relieve muscular tension and spasms. Place both hands on either side of the dog's body or leg and slowly lift upwards for 1–2cm (½–1in). Hold for about 4 seconds, slowly come back down, then slowly release. Lift enough to support the muscle lightly; too much pressure may cause the dog to hold his breath.

The Butterfly Use this light movement alongside the Python Lift to increase circulation. The thumbs are pointed upwards with the fingers wrapped around the dog's leg. Lift the skin and muscle of the dog in the same way as for the Python Lift. Concentrate on moving slowly.

Tarantulas Pulling the Plow Use light, nimble movements to gently roll the skin, working in a smooth pathway across the dog's shoulders, back and sides.

Belly Lifts Start behind the front legs and lift the dog's abdomen. Hold for 10–15 seconds, depending on the reaction. It is important that the pressure is released slowly and takes more time than the lift. Move gradually along the body towards the flank and repeat. Go as close to the flank as is comfortable for the dog: some dogs are very ticklish in this area, especially when in pain. Two people can work the movement holding a towel between them; one person working alone can use his forearms and hands.

Back Lifts With fingers apart and curved upwards, start on the far side of the belly in the middle. In a raking motion, bring both hands across the belly and partway up the barrel of the body. Start gently and increase the pressure if the animal doesn't respond. You should be able to see the top of the back rise upwards.

Physical therapies: reiki

holistic dog care

Reiki is a hands-on therapy that bridges the gap between the physical therapies of massage and TTouch, and the pure energy therapies. It involves hand placements and movements, which are designed more to direct the healing energies to strengthen the spirit or repair an injured area than to stimulate the skin and tissues themselves.

It is said that the healing energy of Reiki was first used in India by Buddha and later in the Middle East by Jesus. Its secrets were lost over the years but were rediscovered in the late 19th century by a Japanese doctor, Dr Mikao Usui. It is said that when the doctor was close to death from cholera,

he joined a Zen monastry and was taught the thoery of Reiki. Practical knowledge of the application came to him in a vision, when he was shown symbols from the sutra and was taught how to use them. He was also given the ritual of attunement, which allows Reiki knowledge to pass from the initiated master to the uninitiated student. These rituals are still used in Reiki today.

The name Reiki is thought to originate from two Japanese symbols, "Rei" meaning universal and "Ki", the non-physical life force. (Ki is similar to Q'i in acupuncture, the Vital Force of life.) The powerful healing energy, Ki, is freely available to those who

are able to use it. Unfortunately, most of us are disconnected from it because of the stress and isolation of modern life. Reiki aims to reconnect people to life's energy force, so enabling them to heal themselves, their family and friends, and their animals.

There are three degrees of Reiki. In the First Degree the student is attuned to the life-force and can begin to channel it where it is needed. The student is also taught the hand placements and movements that are essential to direct the energy to the patient. In the Second Degree the student is taught the symbols and mantras that allow the energy to be focused more strongly on the

SOME HAND POSITIONS FOR TREATING DOGS

Choose one of the following to give your dog the benefit of a Reiki experience at any time.

If your dog is suffering physical or emotional distress, be sensitive to his response and stop treatment immediately if he appears to resent it. Do not place your hands directly on areas of acute inflammation, but hold your hands parallel to and just above the damaged area.

• Hold your hands either side of the ribcage, with the dog seated on your lap or in front of you on the floor. This will treat the whole body and the Reiki will reach central parts immediately.

• Put one hand on the head of your dog as though you are going to stroke its ears, and one hand very lightly on the middle of the dog's back.

• Hold the dog between your hands, with one hand at the top of the spine and one by its tail at the base of the spine.

△ **If the dog's leg is broken, do not place hands directly over the injury. Placing one hand on the dog near to the injury will help to take away the pain. The other hand should be held over the adrenals in order to energize the dog's response to stress. It is important to keep the palms parallel to the dog's body.**

△ Cupping your hands around the dog's ears will redirect the energy flow of the bud chakra at the base of the ears to benefit the dog.

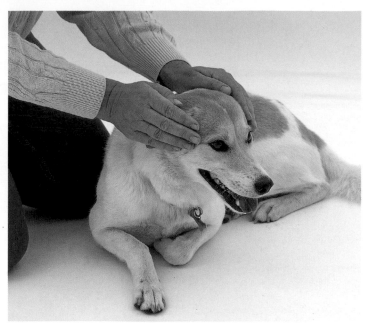

△ Giving the dog a whole body treatment will direct the flow of energy where it is most needed. Start at the top of the head with your hands over the bud chakra energy channel at the base of the dog's ears. Work from the head down the neck, back, abdomen and legs, and always end with the feet.

patient. It is also possible to use these for distant healing. The Third Degree, or Reiki Master level, is the teaching level. Knowledge of this degree is passed from master to student on a one-to-one level.

Because Reiki energy connects all life, it is universal and is used to heal dogs in the same way as it is used on humans. Reiki can be used on dogs as an uplifting tonic or to ease actual suffering. Place your hands comfortably on the dog or over an injury or wound; the dog will move away or appear restless when it has had enough of the treatment. Reki can also be used to reassure dogs who are emotionally upset.

Reiki should not be used as the only means of treating a sick animal. If your dog appears ill, have him looked at by a vet and use Reiki to support the prescribed treatment, including surgery. The main use of Reiki should be to keep your dog in a state of optimum health and to prevent serious disease becoming established.

▷ Reiki can be used on a sick dog to support conventional treatment, and will help to reduce the stress of physical injuries, such as hip displasia. Where the dog is experiencing acute pain, move slowly and with relaxed movements: most dogs are frightened when in pain, and even a mild-mannered dog is less predictable.

Medicinal therapies: herbalism

Herbalism is probably the oldest form of healing still in use today. Herbal medicines are an essential part of the ancient medical systems of Traditional Chinese Medicine and the Indian Ayurvedic system. Western herbalism dates back to the ancient Greeks. It was the mainstay of English medicine until the 1930s and the introduction of the sulphonamides, a group of medicines which were the precursor of modern antibiotics.

Herbalism is now making a resurgence, caused in part by an increasing suspicion that the long-term effects of some modern drugs may not be totally beneficial to the patient. This suspicion is prompting a reappraisal of all medical therapies and is encouraging an interest in holistic medicine and a desire for safe natural medicines, for both humans and animals, which do not involve toxins or side effects. The fact that dogs and other animals are known to seek out and eat plants that are known to have medicinal properties supports the view that herbalism should have an established place in orthodox veterinary medicine.

Many people take the view that as plants are natural, and natural products must be safer than manufactured ones, herbalism is therefore totally safe. This is not the case. Some plants are poisonous in their natural form, and herbal medicines derived from an original plant source can be toxic if given in overdose. Always check the toxicity of your chosen plant.

CONDITION	HERBAL THERAPY
Cancer prevention	lemon balm; mistletoe leaf; barberry bark; roman chamomile flower; comfrey leaf; echinacea root; fenugreek seed
Itchy skin	German chamomile flower; burdock root; curled dock root; liquorice root; southernwood
Skin abrasions	turmeric root; yarrow; peppermint; comfrey leaf
Colitis	marsh mallow root; nutmeg seed; turmeric seed
Heart disease	hawthorn; motherwort; dandelion leaf
Urinary tract disorders	stone root; field horsetail; couch grass; bearberry leaf; juniper berry; marsh mallow root
Kidney impairment	cinnamon bark; rehmannia root; comfrey leaf; celery seed

Some pharmacists object to the use of herbalism. This is because the chemical composition of individual plants of the same species varies according to the soil they are grown in and the season of the year in which they are harvested. This means that medicines derived from plants are by no means standardized. This is compounded according to which part of the plant is used and the method of extraction used on that plant material. Pharmacists would prefer to isolate the part of the plant that they consider to be the active ingredient, and

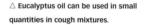

eucalyptus

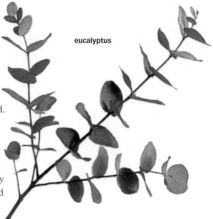

△ Eucalyptus oil can be used in small quantities in cough mixtures.

▷ Herbal teas and decocotions can be stored for at least 2 days in a well stoppered bottle.

◁ Herbal teas are best given through the side of the mouth, but not all dogs appreciate them as much as this one does.

one drop per 13kg (5lb) of body-weight. Herbal capsules and tablets are now being made for canine use, but some authorities believe that capsules of powdered herbs are not suitable for carnivorous animals. If using them, buy from a reputable firm and follow the instructions carefully. Bulk herbs can also be used to make poultices and compresses. Do not use toxic herbs in this way as a dog is likely to lick the dressing and it may poison itself.

There are very few practising veterinary herbalists. Some vets undertake courses in herbalism to combine it with their veterinary knowledge. They can then carefully treat animals, monitoring their response to treatment before increasing the dose. With experience, their dosing regimes are becoming more accurate.

In cases of minor illness you can treat the dog with herbs yourself. Keep up the treatment for one week before rejecting it as ineffective. In cases of chronic disease it can take longer for improvement to be seen, although in these situations herbalism is best used to support conventional care. The health of the dog is paramount; if the dog's condition appears to deteriorate, stop the treatment and consult your vet.

use only that ingredient in a purified form. This is the only way to know exactly what action a single dose of medicine has on the body.

Unfortunately, few active agents have only one effect. They tend to have other unwanted actions or side effects. Herbalists believe that the active ingredients of herbal medicines work together to counteract harmful side effects. This allows a safe, effective dosage to be made.

Herbal medicines can be given in many forms. The traditional method is in the form of herbal teas, which are made from bulk herbs that are available in loose form. Like all herbal preparations, bulk herbs should always be purchased from reputable firms.

Herbal teas for dogs are made in the same way as they are for humans. The difference seems to be that dogs appear to need more in relation to their body weight than humans. A dose of 20ml (4tsp) twice a day is generally accepted as suitable for a dog weighing about 50kg (20lb). Good-tasting bulk herbs can be fed directly to the dog if mixed with its food.

Commercial herbal extracts in the form of glycerine/water and alcohol/water tinctures are available from reputable suppliers and can be given directly into the mouth of some dogs. Here, the dose rate is

▷ Commercial extracts are standardized and will have a more constant effect than home-made teas. They can also be stored for longer periods.

Medicinal therapies: aromatherapy

Aromatherapy is the use of volatile aromatic oils, which are derived from plant material, to cause physiological and psychological changes in the patient. The molecules of these essential oils are able to enter the body and the bloodstream by absorption through the lining of the nose and lungs or through the skin. This means that aromatherapy oils are as much medicinal substances as any conventional drug taken by mouth or given by injection.

Fragrant oils have been used medicinally in the Middle East, for thousands of years. Their use is not taught in medical or veterinary schools at present, although some holistic veterinary clinics use aromatherapy, as do some human hospitals.

Several parts of the plant can be used as a source of the essential oil. The flowers, leaves, twigs, roots, seeds, bark and heartwood may be used according to the plant from which the oil is being extracted. There are several methods of extracting the oils, the commonest being steam-distillation. This yields an oil and water mix that is cooled and separated into its two components. Pressing is used to squeeze the oil out of plants containing non-volatile oils. Carbon dioxide extraction is sometimes used but is more expensive. Enfleurage is the traditional process of leaving petals on layers of fat for up to three weeks. During this time the oils seep into the fat, from which they are separated by extraction with alcohol. It is used for extracting delicate flower-oils, such as rose and jasmine. It produces fine oils but is very expensive. Solvent extraction produces oils known as

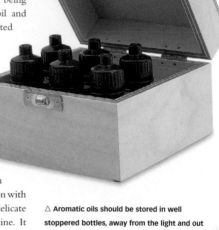

△ Aromatic oils should be stored in well stoppered bottles, away from the light and out of contact with homeopathic remedies, or inquisitive children or pets.

▷ Essential oils should never be used undiluted on the dog's skin. Blend with a carrier oil before using oils for massage.

absolutes, which may contain traces of the solvent. For this reason they are disliked by some therapists. Synthetic oils are also produced. They are a much more standardized product but are thought not to contain all the many components of the natural oil, which may reduce their therapeutic effect. They are thought by some therapists not to be as active as natural oils because they have a non-living chemical source which is devoid of the vitality of living materials.

There are hundreds of component oils in every extract. The final contents are governed by the geographical area and the soil in which it is grown, the climate, and the methods used in cultivation. Organically-grown plants should be used to eliminate contamination with agrochemicals. Choose your supplier with care, and regard cheap oils with suspicion, although expense does not necessarily indicate good quality.

CONDITION	ESSENTIAL OIL
Lack of confidence, anxiety, panic	ylang ylang, sandalwood
Loneliness, fear of being alone	basil, bergamot or orange blossom
Restlessness, frustration	chamomile
Liver problems	rosemary
Kidney and bladder problems	juniper
Skin allergies	lavender, pine, terebinth
Respiratory problems	cedarwood, eucalyptus, lemon, tea tree, lavender
Minor wounds and bites and stings	lavender, tea tree
Toothache	clove

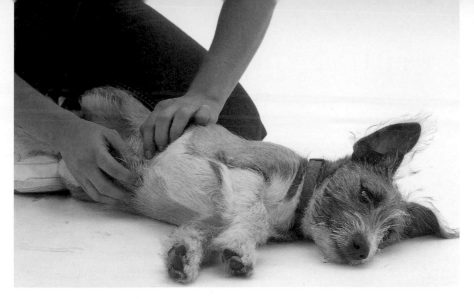

◁ **The relatively bare areas of the belly, groin and armpit are the best sites for the application of essential oils by massage.**

lavender sprig

◁ **Lavender oil is widely used for skin wounds and insect bites, but should not be applied directly to damaged skin.**

The dog has a highly developed sense of smell and can be expected to respond well to aromatherapy. Dogs instinctively use the secretions of their anal sacs and the glands of their feet, tails and cheeks, along with saliva, urine and faeces as a means of communication. This is to identify themselves, both for attracting mates and possibly deterring aggressors. It means that they should be very suitable candidates for intranasal drug administration.

Administration by massage is not really suitable for dogs except in the less hairy regions such as the armpit and groin. Soaking its body in a bath containing a few drops of oil is also unsuitable. It is difficult to get a dog to hold its head over an inhalation of oil in hot water. The best method for a dog is inhalation using a vaporizer. In this method 5–10 drops of oil are floated on water which is being heated by a candle or night-light. The heating causes the oil/water mixture to evaporate and the fragrant vapour fills the room where it is inhaled by everyone, people and pets alike. This makes it suitable for the home treatment of sick dogs, especially those who resist oral medication. Inhalation is not suitable for treatment in a veterinary surgery or hospital because it would mean that other dogs would receive the same treatment, regardless of their symptoms.

Combinations of up to four oils can be used according to the symptoms present. Such combinations should be freshly prepared by a professional aromatherapist. Aromatherapy can be used to support any mainstream or complementary therapy with the exception of homeopathy, because homeopathic remedies can be deactivated by highly aromatic substances.

It must be remembered that essential oils are concentrated chemicals and can be toxic in their neat form. They should never be used undiluted on the animal's skin. As well as absorbing the oil through the skin, the dog will also lick its fur and take in toxic doses through its mouth. Remember that a dog's nose is very sensitive. This may mean that what smells beautiful to a human nose may be unbearably strong for a dog and may not have the desired effect.

▽ **Vapourization is the easiest and gentlest method of using aromatherapy with dogs.**

Medicinal therapies: pharmaceuticals

Even when adopting a holistic approach to health, conventional Western medicine does not need to be abandoned altogether. Acupuncture, herbalism and homeopathy are complete systems of medicine in their own right, but this does not necessarily mean that these systems are equally effective 100 per cent of the time. Each individual is unique, with their own unique response to treatment. Every dog will respond in a different way to the same treatment. Complementary treatments can and do work, and sometimes they are enough in themselves to effect a complete cure. There are also times, however, when modern medicines are needed. They may not be needed as the sole medication but they can form part of an approach using a combination of several therapies.

Modern Western medicine is based on an accurate diagnosis. After the illness has been correctly identified and named, the aim is to find and administer the one, true medicine that will cure the condition. This medicine is the "magic bullet" that will kill the disease. It is a beautiful idea, but unfortunately medicines have more than

one, simple action in the body. Unwanted actions are the side effects of the drug. When medicines are given in short courses of small doses, the body is able to correct any damage which has been done inadvertently by the medicine whilst it heals the disease it was sent to cure. In chronic disease, where medicines are given over longer periods of time, the side effects can overcome the body's ability to deal with them. The original natural disease is now overtaken and made worse by medicine-induced disease. It might be argued that chronic disease is itself an indication that the medicine has not cured but has simply suppressed the symptoms, giving a false impression of a cure.

Many modern medicines are derived by isolating the active ingredient found in herbal medicines. Having isolated and identified the chemical structure of the active ingredient, attempts are then made to synthesize medicines that have a similar structure and a stronger action. These tend to have stronger side effects as well. The first antibiotic, penicillin, was isolated from a fungal culture. Since then, other natural

antibiotics have been found, and synthetics based on the chemical structure of these natural products have been manufactured. However, the side effects of synthetic drugs usually become more serious as each new generation of antibiotics is developed. Scientists have also manufactured synthetic hormones and vitamins, but some of these have proved to be less effective than the natural product.

Modern medicine is at its best in cases where the patient has a mineral deficiency, for example when a bitch develops milk fever after whelping. Injection of a calcium salt solution will remove the symptoms, but it must be followed by dietary changes, preferably backed-up with further support from appropriate homeopathic medicines.

In the case of hormone deficiencies, for example in conditions such as diabetes and the under-activity of the thyroid gland (hypothyroidism), replacement with insulin or thyroid extract is beneficial. Properly supported by an appropriate complementary therapy, the amount of the replacement can be reduced, and sometimes the need for replacement therapy disappears altogether.

▷ **Pharmaceutical preparations come in many forms. They are all standardized to ensure that every dose has the same effect on every patient.**

▽ Veterinary nurses play an important role in a modern, scientific veterinary practice. Their training enables them to advise clients on the modern methods of flea and worm control.

▷ Veterinary nurses are also trained to run obesity clinics and to advise owners on the content and quantity of their dog's diet, and on suitable exercise programmes for weight loss.

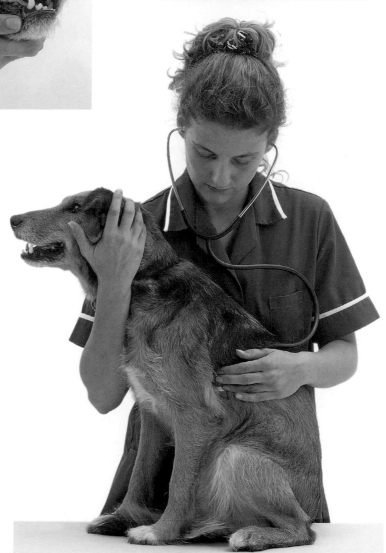

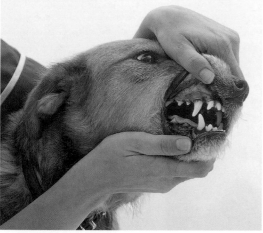

▷ Veterinary nurses monitor heart and lung function as part of a pre-surgery check-up and during operations.

In acute bacterial infections, antibiotics are of great value, but good complementary medicine used alongside antibiotics will allow the use of smaller courses of milder antibiotics than would otherwise be needed. Such a holistic approach will reduce the number and the severity of the side effects experienced by the dog. It will speed convalescence and correct the weakness that enabled the infection to occur in the first place. Steroids are useful when your dog has severe inflammatory conditions (they should only be used in short courses) but complementary support used with antibiotics can provide similar benefits without the need for steroids. With certain forms of cancer, chemotherapy is a valid treatment, although the painful and very distressing side effects of the therapy can be substantially reduced with a sensible holistic treatment plan used in support.

Modern medicine has a genuine place in the treatment of disease. However, used ideally, it should form one part of a holistic approach to your dog's health.

Energy therapies: acupuncture

Acupuncture is part of Traditional Chinese Medicine (TCM), which has been developed by the Chinese for over 3,000 years. It is based on the principle of the flow of energy, "Q'i", (pronounced "chee") around the body through non-anatomical channels known as "meridians". If the flow of Q'i passing through any of these channels is disturbed, the health of the body is impaired, which leads to disease.

The body's energy flow increases and decreases in each meridian in a fixed cycle. These meridians also govern the function of an anatomical unit, although their function in TCM is different to Western medicine.

Q'i has two opposite but complementary components: "yin" and "yang". Everything in the universe contains yin and yang, but some things contain more yin than yang and vice versa. The solid organs of the body – liver, spleen, kidney, heart, lungs and pericardium – are yin, while the hollow organs – stomach, small and large intestines, gall bladder and urinary bladder – are yang. One pair of meridians governs each organ, and there are two other non-paired meridians, the Governing Vessel and the Conception Vessel. These meridians run in pathways up the front and down the back of the body.

Acupuncture theory holds that every-thing in the universe is made from five basic philosophical elements: wood, fire, earth, metal and water. These elements relate in a positive or negative way to one another, so that wood produces fire, but restrains or destroys earth. Each element can change to the next in the course of a creative cycle.

Chinese acupuncture recognizes six environmental factors as the principal reasons for disease: wind, cold, summer heat, dampness, dryness and heat; each is associated with certain forms of disease. It also recognizes eight conditions composed of four pairs of opposites: yin and yang, internal and external, heat and cold, and excess and deficiency. The theory is that all disease is expressed by a combination of these eight conditions.

In acupuncture, no medicines are given, although Chinese herbs may be used in support of the treatment. Treatment itself is based on stimulating precise anatomical positions along the meridians. These positions are based on the monitored results of stimulation over thousands of years. In the beginning, finger-pressure was used, and later, thin slivers of bamboo or bone were inserted into underlying tissues. Today, fine surgical steel needles are used. The relationships between

△ In the West, acupuncture treatment begins with a thorough examination of the dog in order to make a correct diagnosis of the problem.

the five elements, the six environmental factors and the eight conditions of opposites indicate which points on which meridian should bring Q'i back into balance and allow the body's natural healing forces to complete the cure.

There is no bodily structure or organ recognized by Western anatomists that is penetrated by needles and which could be responsible for the definite physical and physiological changes that result from treatment. The effects of acupuncture can-not be explained in physical or biochem-ical terms, which suggests that they occur at a different level, somewhere in the invisible, energetic bodies that surround the physical level known to Western science. For many

---

CONDITIONS THAT RESPOND BEST TO ACUPUNCTURE

• Musculoskeletal problems: arthritis, disc problems, hip displasia, spinal problems, lameness
• Chronic gastrointestinal diseases: chronic digestive disturbances such as chronic
   diarrhea or vomiting, distemper
• Neurological problems: nerve deafness, nerve injuries, epilepsy and some types of
   paralysis
• Skin diseases and allergic dermititis
• A variety of other problems, such as chronic pain syndrome, breeding problems,
   respiratory arrest and coma

Note: Acupuncture is not recommended for healing dogs with cancer as it may unwittingly
stimulate the disease

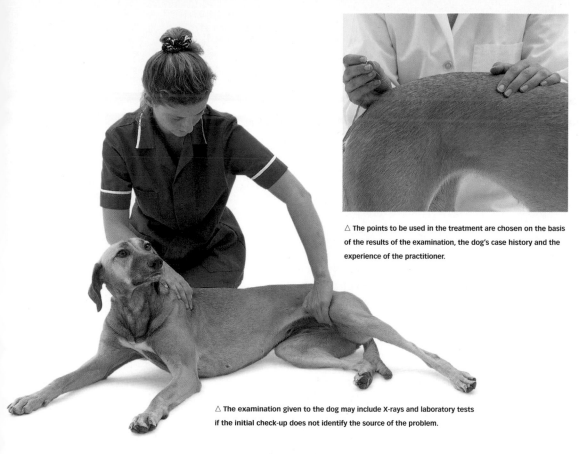

△ The points to be used in the treatment are chosen on the basis of the results of the examination, the dog's case history and the experience of the practitioner.

△ The examination given to the dog may include X-rays and laboratory tests if the initial check-up does not identify the source of the problem.

conventional Western-trained physicians, the philosophy of acupuncture and its approach to treatment is hard to evaluate. A form of acupuncture has been developed in the West which uses fixed combinations of points for each diagnosis. It is empirical, but the essential art of acupuncture has been lost. It cannot be used on as many conditions and the results are inferior. Therefore, references throughout this book are to traditional Chinese acupuncture.

Since Q'i, the philosophical elements, environmental factors and conditions of acupuncture are universal, its theory can be applied as easily to dogs as to humans. The positions of the meridian and acupuncture points varies from species to species, but the same positions can be used on dogs and humans alike. Your dog is not likely to resist treatment. Most dogs find the therapy relaxing, and some have been known to fall asleep while the needles are in place.

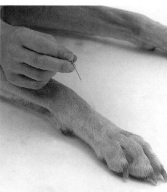

As a therapy, acupuncture is not as good as antibiotics at dealing with acute infections, but it is very good with chronic diseases, including diseases of the immune system. Acupuncture is not for home use. Ask your vet to refer you to a qualified practitioner if you are interested in using it on your dog.

◁ Needles are placed at various depths, dependng on the size of the dog and the treatment being given.

acupressure

The use of needles is reserved by law to vets but, if you want to provide back-up care for your dog, simple training from a qualified practitioner will allow you to perform finger pressure, or "acupressure", at home to support conventional treatment.

Like acupuncture, acupressure is based on the principle of Q'i, and is said to reduce pain by relaxing the muscles. It is applied with light finger-tip or finger-nail pressure on the acupuncture points; some styles of acupressure also involve rubbing, kneading and rolling. Acupressure done incorrectly can increase pain, however. As with all therapies, do not proceed if your dog dislikes the treatment.

Energy therapies: homeopathy

Homeopathy was the first holistic system of Western medicine to be developed. It can be very effective both on its own and in support of conventional medicine and, like acupuncture, it is at its best where conventional medicine is weakest.

The body has a natural healing force, which is implemented in cases of illness or injury: small cuts and grazes heal on their own, and we soon get over minor coughs and colds. Scientists call this healing force "homeostasis", and homeopaths believe that their medicine stimulates it. Samuel Hahnemann, an 18th-century German doctor and the originator of homeopathy, called the animal impulse for self-healing the Vital Force. He saw it as an energetically active, living force, which is essential to life. He took large doses of extract of *Chincona* bark (the tree from which quinine is extracted), and from his observations he deduced that a non-lethal quantity of a poison can stimulate healing of any disease whose symptoms are similar to the effects of that poison.

The idea that like cures like dates back to the ancient Greeks, but had never before been used as the basis for a medical therapy. Hahnemann tested substances on himself and his friends, and recorded the results in a volume he called the *Materia Medica*.

Hahnemann at first used small, material doses, and found that some patients got worse before they got better, a phenomenon he called "homeopathic aggravation". To reduce the aggravations, he reduced the size of the dose, but although diluting reduced the aggravations, it also reduced the benefits. Next, liquid medicines were shaken after dilution in a method known as "potentizing". This reduced the aggravations while, at the same time, it enhanced the healing property of the medicines or "potencies".

WHEN TO USE HOMEOPATHY

Remedies are available in different potencies, of which the most common are *6C* and *30C*. Use *6C* potency for common or long-standing ailments, and *30C* potency for emergencies and chronic symptoms.

CONDITION	REMEDY
Panic attacks and emotional stress	Aconite
Prolonged grief	Ignatia
Flea bites and wasp stings	Apic
Bruises and swelling	Arnica
Flatulence and digestive disorders	Carbo Veg
Skin grazes and superficial wounds	Hypercium
Physical exhaustion	Arnica

◁ Homeopathic remedies come in the same form as more conventional medicines. To the casual observer, there is no difference in appearance between one homeopathic preparation and the next.

The potentizing process is unique to homeopathy. At each stage there are two procedures: the dilution in a fixed ratio of 1:9 or 1:99, and the succussion of the diluted solution by vigorous shaking. This is essential if the medical effects of the solution are to be enhanced or potentized as the concentration is reduced.

The starting point of a potency is the saturated solution of a soluble chemical, or the alcoholic extract of plant material known as the "mother tincture". Each succeeding potency is given a number for the number of dilutions made, and a letter for the Latin number of the degree of dilution, *X* or *D* standing for 10, *C* for 100, and *LM* for 50,000. For example, if you put one drop of the mother tincture of *Belladonna* with 99 drops of alcohol/water and succuss it, you get a *1C* potency. One drop of the *1C* potency mixed with 99 drops of alcohol/water gives a *2C* potency, and one drop of a *2C* potency mixed with 99 drops of alcohol/water gives a *3C* potency, and so on. Potencies up to *30C* are still made by hand, and to these is added the suffix *H* for Hahnemann. Potencies from *30C* to *10M* are usually produced by mechanical methods.

The use of highly diluted medicines has led to two misconceptions. First, that the essence of homeopathy is the use of a very small dose rather than the use of a similar. Second, that because there are no molecules left in potencies above *12X* or *6C*, the medicine could not possibly work. Observations over the last 200 years, however, have shown that these medicines do affect the living body. This phenomena is under scientific study, but the method by which homeopathy achieves its results will probably prove to be sub-atomic, at an energetic level. Like acupuncture, homeopathy is as applicable to sick dogs as to ailing humans.

A similar is the medical agent with symptoms closely resembling those of the dog, and if the symptoms match completely, it is the similimum. When a dog is treated, its physical, mental, and emotional reactions to the world are used to identify the disease. The totality of the animal and its condition is treated, and the more you know about your dog in health, the more you can help . The smallest dose of the similimum that will stimulate the healing process is given. In acute cases, doses are repeated until benefits are seen. In chronic cases, each dose is left to have its full effect before it is repeated.

△ **The gentle action of homeopathic remedies is always appreciated by the patient.**

The second branch of homeopathic treatment is the removal of obstructions to a cure. This relates to the modern holistic idea that unless there is suitable nutrition, hygiene, living conditions and lifestyle, a complete and permanent cure is unlikely to result, no matter what the medicine. A good homeopath should enquire about these factors and give appropriate advice.

Tissue salts make up the third branch of homeopathy. In the 19th century, a German homeopathic doctor, Wilhelm Schüssler, identified twelve basic salts in the body and developed the idea that, if caught early and without complex symptoms, all disease could be treated with a combination of the twelve salts. Biochemic tissue salts are often prescribed by homeopathic vets for use in low *6X* potencies to alleviate mild physical or emotional disease conditions, which may be caused by a mineral salt deficiency. Nutritional advice will also be given as part of the treatment.

▽ **Dogs will normally take powdered tablets without complaint. If it does object, the powder can be stirred into the drinking water.**

WHEN TO USE TISSUE SALTS	
CONDITION	**REMEDY**
Emotional stress	Kali phos.
Allergies	Nat. sulph.
Neurological disorders	Silica
Dental problems	Calc. fluor.

Energy therapies: Bach Flowers

Plants and flowers play an essential part in many traditional healing systems. Flower essences, prepared from the stalks, petals and leaves of plants, can be used in response to canine emotional states.

The German homeopath Dr Samuel Hahnemann discovered a way of using the vibrational energy of plants to stimulate natural healing processes in his holistic system of homeopathy. A bacteriologist from Britain, Dr Edward Bach, took Hahnemann's ideas one stage further. His experience as a homeopathic doctor had convinced him that physical disease was the result of the body's reaction to a non-material cause. Changes in the body's fundamental vibrational energy (what the acupuncturist calls Q'i and what the homeopath calls the Vital Force) resulted in a pathological change of mental state that could eventually lead to physical disease.

To Dr Bach, it appeared that mental attitude was more important in the choice of a medicine than physical symptoms. He believed that the mind showed the onset

and cause of disease much more definitely and much sooner than the body. He closed his Harley Street practice in London in 1930, at the age of 43, to seek a means of healing that used non-toxic materials rather than potentized poisons.

Dr Bach was a sensitive, spiritual man, who noted that his own moods could be influenced by the plants that he came into contact with. He started to look towards individual plants for his remedies, and his theory was that the natural vibrations of certain plants responded to the natural vibrations associated with certain mental states. Therefore, if the plants were appropriately prepared, they may be able to correct distorted vibrations by the principle of resonance.

Initially, Bach used his intuition to discover 12 plants which affected pathological mental states. Later he increased the range to 37 plants, plus *Rock Water,* which is water from a natural spring (preferably a spring reputed to have healing properties). He also sanctioned the use of a combination of five remedies in a preparation called *Rescue Remedy.*

△ Floating fresh flowers on 300ml (½ pint) of spring water in bright sunlight will yield 600ml (1 pint) of mother tincture when diluted with brandy. This is how the remedies are prepared.

Rescue Remedy is the most popular essence for dogs, and is used in emergency situations for panic, shock and hysteria.

Bach chose two methods of preparation for his plants, based on the seasons. Flowers of plants which bloomed in the late spring and summer were picked at about 9.00 a.m. on sunny days. The flowers were floated on 300ml (½ pint) of spring water in a glass bowl and left in sunlight. If the sun clouded over, the batch was discarded. The flowers were removed using stems or branches of the same flower so that the energized water was not contaminated by human touch. This energized water was used to fill bottles half-full of brandy. This was the mother tincture. Two drops of this added to 30ml (2 tbsp) of brandy gave what Bach called the stock solution.

Plants that bloomed in the late winter and spring were processed by the boiling method. The flowers and stems were again picked on a bright, sunny morning before

▷ Only two drops of mother tincture are needed to produce 30ml (2 tbsp) of a stock solution that is further diluted before it is given to the patient.

△ Flowers must be picked in bright, early morning sunshine if the mother tincture is to work. Wild flowers are preferred, and all flowers should be free of pollutants. Human contact with the flowers should be minimal.

△ Winter and early summer twigs, leaves and flowers are processed by the boiling method and need to be simmered gently for at least 30 minutes to produce an effective mother tincture.

9.00 a.m. They were collected in a saucepan, and when the pan was three-quarters full, the lid was fitted and the material was taken home. The flowers and stems were covered with about 1.2 litres (2 pints) of spring water and simmered for 30 minutes, uncovered. The lid was then replaced and the covered pot put outside to cool. When cool, the stems were removed using twigs of the same plant, and the liquid filtered and used to make the mother tincture, as before.

The plants used for the remedies are ideally wild ones growing in unpolluted areas. If cultivated plants have to be used, they should be organically grown to avoid contamination with toxic chemicals. *Rock Water* (or "holy" spring water) should be free from agrochemicals. Flowers from several plants should be used, rather than the flowers of one plant alone.

Flower medicines can be prepared for the patient, although single remedies are now available in health-food stores and some chemists for use at home. Up to five remedies can be combined depending on the patient's needs, using two drops of each essence in 30ml (2 tbsp) of spring water.

Bach Flowers are particularly valuable for behaviour problems, and while clinical tests have proved inconclusive in explaining how and why they work, positive results have been seen in both humans and dogs. The medicines are chosen according to the dog's mental state, using human emotions as a guide. The owner talks in detail to the therapist about the dog's usual temperament. Treatment is based on the pathological mental state of the dog and not on the nature of its inappropriate behaviour.

Dr Bach believed his remedies covered all known emotional states. More recently, however, other series of flower essences have been developed, such as Californian and Australian Bush flower remedies. These have been developed with modern life in mind, and offer treatments for such factors as the ill effects of pollution and stress. These remedies are prepared and used in the same way as the Bach Flowers, and although they can be used on animals, they are perhaps less relevant for dogs than for humans.

STATE OF MIND	FLOWER REMEDY
Shyness	Mimulus
Apathy	Wild Rose
Fear on behalf of the family	Red Chestnut
Lack of self-confidence	Larch
Lack of concentration	Clematis
Melancholy	Mustard
Aloofness	Water Violet
Excessive desire for companionship	Heather
Over-protectiveness	Chicory
Dominance	Vine

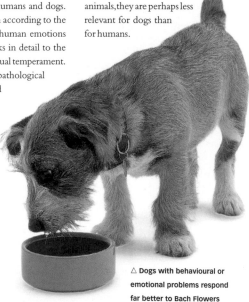

△ Dogs with behavioural or emotional problems respond far better to Bach Flowers than to pharmaceutical drugs.

Energy therapies: crystal therapies

Crystals have been used for healing purposes for thousands of years. They have a regular, fixed, atomic structure as opposed to the chaotic arrangement of atoms in non-crystalline material. The natural energy of the atoms is harmonized by this structure and every crystal has a natural frequency of vibration. This regularity is so stable that it is used to control electric clocks and the frequencies of radio receivers and transmitters. The vibration frequency of crystals is also a source of electrical energy, as demonstrated by the crystal radio sets of the 1930s.

Empirical studies indicate that through harmonic resonance the vibrational energy of a crystal can affect the basic energetic vibration of both people and animals. The energy of the crystal is believed to enter the body through the chakras, or energy-centres of the body, of Ayurvedic medicine. Each chakra is related to a hormone-producing gland of the body, and each has its own harmonic colour vibration.

◁ Placing your hand over the major chakra at the crown of the dog's head will help to redirect the energy flow back into the body to restore a sense of equilibrium in the dog.

In turn, these correspond to seven layers or energy bands in the aura – the invisible energy field that surrounds the physical body – which have been studied and identified over thousands of years. Because of the universality of life-energy, these factors are as valid for animals as they are for humans. The only difference is the location of the chakras within the physical body. They have been accurately mapped in humans, but the correspondencies are not exactly the same for animals. There is some controversy over the location of the minor and bud chakras in dogs, although there is general agreement about the major chakras.

As with the Bach Flowers, the mental state of the patient is the major factor in choosing which crystals should be used. Some crystals seem to have an affinity for certain body systems or symptoms. The factors quoted for crystal selection for humans can be applied to dogs.

Once the appropriate crystals have been selected, they are placed on the patient's resting body in set patterns. For a dog, the crystals can be taped to its collar or harness; special harnesses are now available with pockets to hold crystals over the appropriate chakra for optimum healing. It is also possible to use liquefied crystal essences, which are produced in a similar way to the flower essences and can be successfully used for mental and emotional problems.

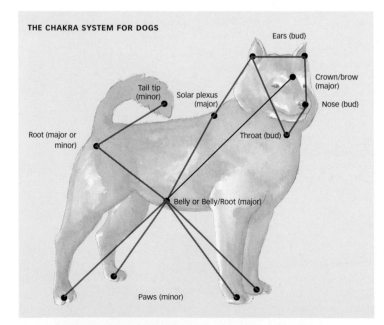

THE CHAKRA SYSTEM FOR DOGS

Ears (bud)

Crown/brow (major)

Nose (bud)

Tail tip (minor)

Solar plexus (major)

Throat (bud)

Root (major or minor)

Belly or Belly/Root (major)

Paws (minor)

Crystals can also be used in light therapy. Light is shone through coloured crystal filters in a darkened room on to the dog's body; the light is directed on to a chakra, an acupuncture point, or the region of the affected organ. Colours have long been known to affect the mind and, increasingly, this phenomena is used when choosing colour schemes for high-stress areas such as medical centres, hospitals and police cells.

Crystals contain metallic ions which can benefit the body's metabolic system. These are slowly absorbed by the body through the skin, if the crystal is in contact with it, in a similar way to the essential oils used in aromatherapy. It has been demonstrated that if a human holds a crystal in the hand for more than 30 minutes the brain waves change from the alert *beta* waves to the more relaxed *alpha* waves. The deep relaxation pattern associated with *theta* and *delta* waves will increase if the crystals are held for periods of more than half an hour.

While crystals emanate healing vibrations, they also absorb negative and pain vibrations from the patient, and to maintain the healing potential of crystals it is necessary to cleanse them regularly. They can be left outside for a 24 hour period when the moon is above the horizon: the dual action of sunlight and moonlight over this period is said to cleanse the crystal. Alternatively, the crystal can be stood in salt-water for 24 hours and then left point downwards for eight hours to dry. Iron-containing crystals can be cleansed using spring water in the same way. Porous crystals, such as lapis lazuli and moonstone, should not be washed. They can be buried for 24 hours and then wiped clean using spring water, if necessary.

citrine quartz   amythyst   rose quartz

CHOOSING CRYSTALS

Amethyst a healing stone to calm the mind

Bloodstone to heal and energize the physical body

Citrine quartz an energizing stone, physically and mentally

Clear quartz for general well-being

Lapis lazuli releases stress to focus and calm

Moonstone clears tension from the emotions and abdomen

Rose quartz to balance the emotions

Rutilated quartz to aid the healing of torn or broken tissue

Smoky quartz a grounding stone and a deep cleanser

Tiger's eye a practical, stable and stimulating energy

Crystal healing is very helpful for dogs whose illness is due to mental and emotional problems, and it can be used to complement all physical medical therapies. However, it is not advised to use crystal therapy on unset broken bones, or before surgery of any kind, because it can interfere with the anaesthetic. Crystal therapists should always discuss the case with the vet before treatment is started and only proceed with the vet's approval.

▷ **To treat your dog with crystals, ask him to lie down and scatter the crystals on the floor around him. Attach the crystals to the dog's collar if the dog becomes restless.**

Treating your dog

The pleasure of keeping a dog brings with it the responsibility of ensuring the dog's lifestyle is as good as it can be. If the dog becomes ill, it is your responsibility to see that it receives the best possible treatment.

As the owner, you have the legal right to treat your dog yourself, although the law insists that the diagnosis and treatment of dogs must be done by, or under the supervision of, a qualified vet. This means that you can treat your dog yourself provided that you discuss the treatment first with a vet. This is particularly important if there is chronic disease and the dog is suffering.

In mild cases, some of the therapies discussed in this book are suitable for home treatment. The use of modern pharmaceuticals is restricted by law to medically-trained professionals. Likewise, the practice of acupuncture, osteopathy and chiropractic must be left to qualified therapists. Herbalism is a borderline case. Simple Western herbalism is a home therapy using proprietary veterinary remedies available from health-food shops and some pet shops.

Traditional Chinese herbalism, on the other hand, must be left to trained practitioners. As with self-help treatments for use on humans, the basic rule has to be if you are in any doubt, consult a trained professional.

The remaining therapies can be used at home with a self-taught knowledge of the therapy. Introductory courses in TTEAM and TTouch are held, as are courses in homeopathy and the veterinary use of Bach Flower remedies. Courses for using massage, Reiki or crystal therapy on dogs are hard to find. However, the therapies are energetically based, and they can be adapted from use on humans with a little common sense.

If your dog displays mood swings, or emotional problems, or signs of behavioural problems, try the therapy with which you are most familiar. If the dog shows mild physical symptoms, such as diarrhoea and vomiting, a cough or muscular stiffness, home treatment can be tried. If, however, there is severe pain, blood in any of the bodily discharges, or if the dog does not respond to treatment, you should see a vet.

▷ CLOCKWISE FROM TOP LEFT **Keeping the inside of your dog's ears free from excess hair will allow good ventilation and help prevent problems, while the power of touch alone can alleviate all kinds of hurts and upsets. All breeds make suitable patients for holistic care, although the character of the dog may affect its response. Give your dog time to acclimatize to anything new and don't bombard him with ointments and oils too quickly: sometimes giving him his own space can be just as beneficial.**

You should also see a vet if your dog is suffering the same complaint repeatedly. The vet will then check for a more serious underlying cause; this is one of the reasons why conventional medicine is a necessary part of holistic care.

Some injuries need surgical repair, but after the surgery, holistic support will speed healing. Conditions such as diabetes and hypothyroidism respond quickly to medical veterinary treatment, but complementary support can reduce the amount of medicine needed and may even effect a complete cure.

When you next visit your vet, make a point of asking what the treatment being provided for your dog is designed to do, and ask about possible side effects. Discuss your interest in complementary medicine and ask about any available therapies that could help in your dog's case.

Relatively few vets have practical experience of complementary therapies. This is not a comment on the success of holistic medicine, and you should not let it deter you. Conventional vets all over the world have, for a long time, shown an interest in holistic practice, but the veterinary profession as a whole is still poorly informed on the subject. The aim of both conventional and complementary medicine is essentially the same: to promote and maintain good health, to restore balance that has been lost and, at the end of life, to help smooth the transition from this world to the next.

◁ **Giving your dog the benefit of fish liver oils is just one of the ways you can strengthen your dog's health at home.**

Behavioural problems: dominance

This is the most common problem referred to behavioural clinics. It arises as a result of the dog not knowing its correct place in the family, and mistakenly believing it is the top-dog, or the leader of the household. Because dominance aggression is a mental disease, a holistic approach is very effective. Use the reward system for initiating all activities with your dog.

In the wild, dogs are grouped in packs and the pack leader has first choice of everything: food, mate and sleeping place; and he initiates interaction with inferior dogs. If your dog brings you a toy to play with, he is showing signs of dominant behaviour as he initiated the activity. If you comply with his wishes, you are signalling that he has dominance over you. If you have trained your dog by the reward system you should tell him to sit and stay and to drop the toy. Then praise him. When ready, you can pick up the toy and invite him to play with you. You decide when the session ends.

Dominance aggression develops when the dog becomes socially mature, at around 18–24 months. Early signs may be seen before this, but are often misinterpreted by the owner.

Physical forms of dominant behaviour are pushing, particularly on the head, neck, shoulders and back. If your dog comes to you, pushes you or jumps up and licks your face, he is trying to dominate you and is not just being overfriendly, as many owners think. Your response when this happens should be to command him to sit and stay, praise him, then ignore him for a while – perhaps by putting him outside. Later on, call him and make a fuss of him.

Similarly, you should never give a titbit to a dog that initiates begging procedures. Tell him to sit and stay and ignore him for a while. Dominant animals lead the way, so make sure that you go through doors before the dog and feed him after you have eaten, at a place which is away from the table.

Dominance aggression develops when the dog has been allowed to initiate minor activities, such as playing with a toy, and then is told that it cannot initiate major ones. In the wild, a true dominant dog knows it is superior and does not have to fight. A dog that is unsure of its status must challenge to find out its place in the pack. Dogs have a sequence of body postures, raising their hackles and growling, which usually resolves the problem without resort to violence, and they will try to use the same sequence of postures with humans. To respond to the dog with physical force is to risk attack and is potentially dangerous. As soon as you begin to notice signs of dominance aggression in your dog, long before force is needed to control the animal, seek help and advice from your vet. He will take down full details of the behaviour and will probably prescribe a drug to reduce anxiety in the dog. The vet will recommend a referral to a behavioural specialist, if necessary, to avert the possibility of someone being bitten or injured.

△ The aim of trainer discs is to startle the dog in order to divert its attentions and put an end to the inappropriate behaviour.

▷ Challenges for supremacy in a pack are usually resolved without fighting. An owner should support the stronger dog.

◁ Help from a behaviourist should be sought long before fighting breaks out between two family dogs in the home.

COMPLEMENTARY TREATMENT

TTouch techniques are good for calming anxious dogs. Use wands if necessary for safety reasons. Aromatherapy can be tried using *Ylang-ylang* or *Sandalwood* in a diffuser. A herbal infusion of *Chamomile* can relax impatient animals that become angry and snappish. Proprietary tablets of *Skullcap* and *Valerian* have a calming effect. Homeopathic remedies should be used one remedy at a time in a 30C potency. This should be given twice a day for up to 5 days, then assess the results. Stop or reduce the tablets if improvement is seen. Give *Belladonna* for angry dogs that erupt quickly and tend to bite. *Nux vom* helps irritable dogs that react to noise and suffer from indigestion; *Hyosyamus* is for cases where rage predominates; and *Lycopodium* is useful where the dog is anxious or will bite if cornered where it cannot physically escape. The Bach Flowers can be successful in some cases. Give them singly or in combination, depending on the dog. Use *Holly* for aggression and a tendency to bite in a confrontation, *Cherry Plum* for dogs that fear losing control of a situation, and *Impatiens* for those which are irritable and nervous. For crystal therapy, *Pearl* or *Onyx* in the liquid-gem oral form can be added to the dog's drinking water.

THE DOG'S MAJOR FACIAL EXPRESSIONS

calm: face relaxed, teeth covered, ears pricked

worried: ears back

suspicious: wrinkled brow; ears lowered

defensive: threat stare; lips pulled back

ready to bite: fangs exposed

remorseful: gaze averted, ears part back

THE DOG'S TAIL POSITIONS

questioning

confident

submissive

ready to fight

tentative

calm

Behavioural problems: fear aggression

holistic dog care

An abnormal fear of humans or other dogs can be a cause of aggression in dogs. Anxiety and fear are natural, life-saving emotions. It is only when they develop to an inappropriate degree that they become abnormal. As an example, while it is a natural response to feel fear inside a burning building, it is not natural to be afraid at the sight of a lighted match. Like dominance aggression, fear aggression usually starts to appear at social maturity (between 18–24 months) but early signs may be seen in dogs as young as three months old.

A fearful dog's normal response is to try to escape from a situation where it feels threatened. If confronted by a human where it cannot escape, the dog will communicate its feelings by snapping and growling. It may then urinate, defecate and empty its anal glands. The dog lowers its head and neck, tucks its tail under its body, raises its

hackles and puts its ears back. It may wrinkle its muzzle and retract its lips, showing its teeth, and then start snarling. Meanwhile it will try to back away. If the dog is backed into a corner with no escape and the person continues to advance, the dog will bite.

A dog that has been severely beaten may demonstrate fear aggression when a stranger approaches or reaches out to touch or pat it. Dogs that have undergone painful or upsetting experiences at the vets will very often show fear aggression on subsequent visits to the surgery.

If there is any chance that your dog may injure a human, professional advice from a behaviourist is needed at once. Support with pharmacological sedatives and complementary therapies may also be given. Swapping the dog's collar for a halter-type headcollar will give more physical control over the dog when exercising outdoors.

△ Complementary therapies can bring peace of mind and reduce susceptibility to fear and panic. Homeopathic Lycopodium has been shown to be effective.

◁ Approach with caution a dog that resents being cornered: even with a mild-tempered dog you risk being bitten. Talking calmly to the dog and giving him a clear escape route will help to defuse the situation.

COMPLEMENTARY TREATMENT

Massage with TTouch tehniques will help to give the dog confidence. The use of aromatherapy oils as for dominance agression can be tried – *Ylang-ylang* or *Sandalwood* in a diffuser. A Bach Flower medicine comprising *aspen* for general anxiety, *Cherry Plum* for extreme fears, *Mimulus* for specific fears and *Rock Rose* for terror, can be useful. Homeopathic *Aconite* can be used if the onset can be tied to a specific painful or frightening experience. *Lycopodium* is often useful in German Shepherd Dogs that show the full range of fear-reaction. Give a *30C* tablet twice daily for up to one week initially, and adjust the dosage according to the response.

Behavioural problems: jealousy

Jealousy is another negative emotional state, where the dog becomes over-conscious of its rights and acts to preserve them. These rights may extend to food, territory and people. If early signs of jealousy are seen in young puppies, it can be corrected by the appropriate sit-stay reward training.

Jealousy may appear when a new dog is introduced into the home. It may occur immediately and result in aggression between the dogs, based on disputes over sleeping rights and precedence at meal times. However, it may not show until the younger dog has reached social maturity at two years. Minor but repeated disputes should be taken as a portent of possible future problems, and should be taken seriously. Remember that when a dog pushes against you to get your attention he is not being affectionate, but trying to dominate you into doing what he wants you to do.

A dog may become either jealous of or over-protective towards its owners. This may manifest itself in an attempt to keep other dogs away from the human family by threatening barks and physical force, often biting. Dogs have even been known to get between husband and wife.

Before jealousy develops to the aggressive stage, training using the reward system can correct it. If signs of aggression are seen, then a halter-type headcollar may be useful. Any attempt by the dog to control activities should be ignored; if necessary, put the dog outdoors or into a "bad behaviour corner" until he has calmed down.

If the situation worsens, or if you think that injury to a human or to another dog is likely, then help must be sought from your vet or a behaviourist. Appropriate treatment includes training to reinforce your superiority; the dog may also be given medication to help it accept the retraining.

△ TTouch massage can give a dog reassurance and make it feel more confident of its position in the household. When the dog is well balanced, signs of jealousy disappear.

chicory

▷ Chicory flower essence can reduce jealousy, possessiveness and attention-seeking behaviour. Use with Rescue Remedy to reduce self trauma.

COMPLEMENTARY TREATMENT
Give TTouch to help relax the dog and make it feel more secure. Aromatherapy with *Sandalwood* or *Ylang-ylang* oils can help. The Bach Flowers can be tried: *Chicory* for possessiveness, *Red Chestnut* for overprotectiveness and *Vine* for territorial aggression. Use homeopathic *Lachesis* for an aggressively jealous dog. If two dogs in the same house are fighting, give *Lachesis* to the aggressor and *Staphysagria* (for resentment) to the victim. *Pulsatilla* is useful for dogs that are normally gentle and affectionate, but which begin to push and nudge as signs of dominant behaviour.

Behavioural problems: pining

◁ The grief felt by a dog at the loss of a loved one results in a lack of interest in everyday activities, sometimes including eating and exercise.

Pining is a particular aspect of separation anxiety. It can occur when a dog is put into kennels, or a teenager goes to college, or the dog's elderly owner moves into a nursing home, or when someone in the family dies. The underlying emotion is normally grief at the loss of a loved one's company, but resentment at being treated so unfairly by being abandoned can also occur.

Pining is a common emotional problem in dogs. It usually starts with a loss of appetite and a reluctance to drink. At the same time, the dog loses interest in play and exercise. Dogs seldom starve themselves to death but the loss of thirst may lead to dehydration, and the coat may become greasy along the back. Physical disease is more common where resentment is the main emotion. This may manifest itself either by a loss of housetraining, incontinence and blood in the urine; or a dry red itchy skin condition that usually starts in the groin or belly area.

Orthodox treatment is not particularly effective. Intravenous fluid therapy corrects dehydration, but anabolics and vitamins do not stimulate the appetite of a pining dog. Treatments for skin and bladder conditions act at the physical level, but will not correct the underlying emotional disturbance, and so tend to contribute to a chronic, recurrent problem. However, pining does respond well to complementary therapies, which are the treatment of choice.

◁ Honeysuckle is the Bach Flower remedy for homesickness. Homeopathic capsicum can be tried when there are physical symptoms.

COMPLEMENTARY TREATMENT
TTouch is a particularly good support for pining as it gives the dog a sense of being loved and wanted. In aromatherapy, *Basil*, *Bergamot* or *Orange Blossom* can all be helpful. The Bach Flowers *Heather*, for loneliness, *Honeysuckle*, for home-sickness and *Walnut*, to help the dog adapt to the changed circumstances, can be tried in combination. Homeopathic *Ignatia* is the remedy for grief that results in marked mood changes. *Natrum mur.* works in cases of long-standing grief associated with a greasy skin and a loss of fur that starts near the tailhead and works towards the shoulders like an arrowhead. *Staphysagria* helps where there is resentment shown by symptoms such as a loss of house-training, cystitis (possibly with blood in the urine), or a dry, red, itchy skin that starts in the belly and groin area.

Behavioural problems: destructiveness

Anxiety at being left alone can manifest itself by destructive and noisy behaviour which occurs when the dog is on its own, but never when its owner is present. The dog recognizes clues in the owner's behaviour that she is leaving and may show mild stress symptoms before the owner leaves; these can increase dramatically to unacceptable levels after the dog has been left. These dogs are extremely disturbed and can be difficult to help.

Severe deprivation in early life, or changes in the dog's needs as it ages can be at the root of this syndrome. Sometimes the onset can be pinned down to a severe mental trauma, such as a burglary or house fire. If so, try giving homeopathic *Aconite 30C* twice daily for up to one week, and the Bach Flower *Rescue Remedy* before leaving.

Long-standing or severe cases will need help from both a vet and a behavioural specialist. Treatment will probably include anti-anxiety drugs and a training schedule specifically targeted at reducing the dog's anxiety. One problem with training is that the owner has to be present to train the dog, yet the anxiety only occurs when the owner is absent.

If the trouble is just starting, try ploys such as leaving the radio on whilst you are out, or leaving a tape recorder timed to come on before the abnormal behaviour begins. Changes to your routine will reduce the leaving clues; for example, put on outdoor clothes before settling down to watch the TV; or when you go out to work, take your work-clothes with you but leave the house in leisure clothes. Try making a tape of relaxing music, then play it at weekends and leave it on when you go out. Give the dog a hollow toy that can be filled with treats and which releases them slowly when rolled about. Arrange for a dog-sitter, or a friend or neighbour to come in while you are out and say "hello" to the dog now and again.

▷ **Giving your dog something to do while you are away can help it forget that you are out. Rawhide chews will certainly keep your dog entertained.**

heather

◁ **Noisiness and destructiveness due to loneliness can be helped by a few drops of the Bach Flower remedy, heather.**

◁ **Anxiety can be reduced by altering your behaviour before going out. The dog is less likely to pick up clues if the routine is varied.**

COMPLEMENTARY TREATMENT

TTouch massage can help the dog to relax generally, but do not do this too close to leaving otherwise it can become a trigger action. Collars that spray *Citronella* oil into the dog's face when it barks appear to be unpleasant enough to reduce barking without increasing the dog's anxiety. *Chamomile* aromatherapy oil can be left in a suitable burner, but make sure it is in a place where the dog cannot upset it while you are out. A combination of the Bach Flowers *Cherry Plum* for extreme fear, Heather for loneliness with noisiness and *Rock Rose* for terror can be added to the dog's drinking water. Homeopathic *Argentum nit.*, *Arsenicum*, *Phosphorus* and *Stramonium* can also be useful.

Physical problems: the eyes

A dog's eyes should be clear and bright, the pupils black and round and the membrane that lines the lids (conjunctiva) should be a pleasant salmon-pink colour. The dog has a third eyelid that moves across the eye from the inside to the outside corner. It is barely visible when the eye is fully open but becomes more apparent if the eye is painful, or if the pad of fat behind the eye disappears. If the third eyelid becomes, and remains, visible in the absence of inflammation or discharge, see a vet in case it is the first sign of a chronic wasting disease.

◁ Homeopathic tablets should be handled with care. Store in the phials in which they were bought and discard any that are spilt.

△ Homeopathic remedies used as tinctures are effective and easy to use for inflamed eyes.

discharges, swelling and inflammation

If discharges gather in the corners of the dog's eye, or on the lids, and there is no inflammation, bathe the eye with cold, boiled salt water using 5ml (1 tsp) of salt in 300ml (½pint) of water.

If inflammation occurs and the eye begins to look angry and red, the eye can be bathed in homeopathic *Euphrasia* tincture diluted 1:10 with cold boiled water, or with a herbal infusion of *Golden Seal* made fresh each day. If the eye has not improved after six hours, you should go to the vet.

If the eyelids are swollen and red but there are no discharges, bathe the eyes as for inflammation and give homeopathic *Apis mell. 6C* every two hours until the eyes look better. If there are discharges present, bathe the eyes in a saline solution, as before, and try one of the following homeopathic medicines hourly until an improvement is seen; then gradually reduce the dose: *Arsen. alb. 6C* if the discharge is watery and scalds the hair off the face, *Pulsatilla 6C* if the discharge is bland and creamy, especially if the dog is gentle, or *Kali bich. 6C* if the discharge is thick, green and stringy.

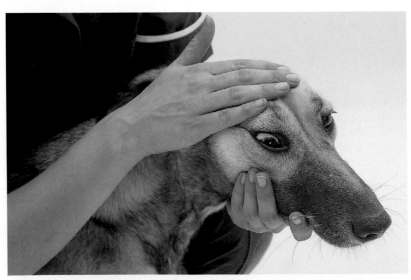

◁ There should be no discharges from the eyes, no nodules on the lids and the conjunctiva should be a healthy salmon pink colour, as seen here.

◁ **The eyes can be cleaned with golden seal infusion, or diluted tincture of euphrasia. Use separate swabs (pads) of cotton wool (cotton balls) for each eye.**

Should the condition not improve, or if it keeps returning, have your vet check the dog for a more serious underlying cause. If none is found, a homeopath may be able to prescribe a constitutional remedy to help the dog, or a tissue salt can be given to restore balance. The following tissue salts may be helpful: *Ferrum phos.* if there are no discharges, *Kali mur.* if there is a white discharge or *Natrum phos.* if the discharge is sticky and yellow.

styes

Styes are infections of the glands in the edge of the eyelid and are very uncomfortable. They can be helped with homeopathic *Silicia 6C* given hourly in most dogs, but *Pulsatilla* may be more successful for gentle, affectionate dogs. If the dog may be harbouring resentment, *Staphysagria* can be very good. Again, bathing the eye twice a day with diluted *Euphrasia* tincture or a *Golden Seal* infusion will support the main medicine prescribed by the vet.

corneal ulcers and glaucoma

If the eye goes cloudy there could be either an ulceration of the cornea (the transparent front of the eyeball) or swelling of the eyeball due to impeded drainage of the eye

itself, a condition known as glaucoma. If an ulcer is left untreated, it can deepen and may eventually rupture, leading to a loss of fluid from the eyeball: the eyeball will then collapse and vision will be lost.

Glaucoma in a dog usually results from a congenital deformity of the eye's drainage apparatus. Inflammation or infection of the inner structures can also interfere with the drainage mechanism. The increase in pressure within the eye results in damage to the retina and loss of vision.

These two conditions are painful and serious and should be seen by a vet as soon as possible. Homeopathic remedies can be used to support conventional treatment. For ulcers the following may be tried: *Argent. nit. 6C* if the dog is anxious, *Acid nit. 6C* if the dog is irritable or aggressive, *Merc. cor. 6C* if the eye is very sore, the dog dislikes the light and the discharge is green, and *Silicia 30C*, used twice daily, to help the last stages of healing. Support the treatment by bathing with *Euphrasia* or *Golden Seal*, as before. For glaucoma, help the dog with *Phosphorus 6C* if it is normally very active and dislikes thunder, or *Spigelia 6C* if the eye is very painful. In all cases, give the tablets hourly to begin with and reduce the dosage if there are signs of improvement.

golden seal

△ **Golden seal has been shown to have antibiotic properties. It is a traditional remedy for eye infections when used as an infusion.**

◁ **The Bach Flower mustard, given orally, can help lift a dog from a state of melancholy brought on by the pain of an infected eye.**

▷

dry eye

Occasionally, the eye stops producing tears, becomes dry and loses its moist appearance, and a thick glutinous mucus gathers over the surface. This condition appears to affect Westies more than any other breed. It can be due to a malfunction of the immune system, an injury to the eye and its surrounding tissues, or a side effect of some drugs, particularly *salizopyrin*. Your vet can test the rate of tear production. If it is low he can prescribe artificial tears to lubricate the eyes. Bathing with cold tea may soothe the eye before the drops are administered, and cod liver oil has been used successfully as a lubricant in mild cases. Homeopathic *Zincum met.* or *Silicia 6C*, used twice daily, has helped, but not cured, some cases.

cataracts

These are opacities in the eye lens which obstruct light from entering the eye, causing blurred vision. They can be present at birth (congenital) or they may develop later in life (acquired). Congenital cataracts do not normally increase in size. Acquired ones come with age or may be associated with diabetes. This type grow slowly and will eventually cause total blindness.

Modern laser treatment is very efficient but it is expensive and should be carried out sooner rather than later, unlike the older surgical method which required the

△ Cold tea can be used to clean dry eyes before three drops (approximately 2.5ml/½ tsp) of cod liver oil are instilled to lubricate them. This Westie, like most dogs, does not mind having his eyes bathed.

cataract to have ripened before surgery was contemplated. Any surgery should be supported with homeopathic *Arnica 6C* given as needed, or *Staphysagria 6C* given four times a day if the dog is prone to resentment. Should surgery be declined on the grounds of the dog's age or the cost, bathing the affected eye with a homeopathic

Cineraria tincture diluted as for *Golden Seal*, may help the dog if daily treatment is maintained for at least three months.

The following homeopathic tablets may help the dog on a constitutional basis. Use the *30C* potency, twice daily, once a week: *Calc. carb.* for elderly, overweight dogs, *Causticum* for withered dogs with lots of

◁ Homeopathic arnica is known to have a beneficial action in support of cataract surgery.

greater celandine

◁ Infusions of greater celandine will help to soothe inflamed eyes, and have been used internally for cataracts.

raspberry leaf

◁ Raspberry leaf is commonly used for its effect on the female reproductive organs. It also has a beneficial effect on inflamed eyes.

warts, or *Silicia* for deeper-chested and thin-limbed dogs, such as Whippets. The tissue salt form of *Silicia* can slow the development of cataracts if given daily, as can herbal infusions of *Greater Celandine* by mouth. Dietary supplements of *Selenium* and *vitamin E* can also help.

districhiasis

Some dogs have two rows of eyelashes, a condition known as districhiasis. The inner row rubs against the front of the eye causing watering and then ulceration. The surgical treatment given for the condition tends to create scarring which can be just as irritating to the eye. Homeopathic *Borax 6C*, given twice daily, has been known to pull the lashes away from the eye.

entropion

Some dogs, especially gun dogs, have eyelids that turn inwards so that the eyelashes rub against the eye. This condition is known as entropion, and conventional treatment is not usually recommended for use on very young dogs. Applying the homeo-pathic remedy *Borax 6C*, as for districhiasis, can delay the need for surgery in puppies until the body is fully grown, and the impact on the adult dog can be properly assessed. In some cases it can prevent the need for any surgery. A herbal infusion of *Rosemary*, given orally twice daily, helps over a long period.

△ Entropion is common in gun dogs, such as this Golden Retriever. Corrective surgery should be delayed until the dog is full grown. Borax or rosemary may help to delay the problem and keep the dog's discomfort to a minimum.

tearducts

These can become blocked by frequent heavy discharges, although some very small dogs are born without them. The result is that tears spill over the lower lid, run down the face and stain the cheek. A vet will test the tearducts by putting a dye into the eye, which should drain into the nose and appear at the nostrils. If it doesn't, the duct is either missing or blocked. If it is missing, nothing can be done except bathe the eye with *Euphrasia* or *Golden Seal*. Conventionally, a blockage is removed under anaesthetic, but the following may also be tried: *Silicia 200C* given twice daily for five days, then weekly, to unblock the duct. The tissue salt *Natrum mur.* can help in long-standing cases.

◁ The facial skin of some dogs is so loose that facelifts are needed to correct drooping eyelids. The St Bernard is a classic example.

Physical problems: the ears

Contrary to conventional thought, most ear conditions are an expression of an internal problem. The size, shape and hairiness of the ear are minor factors in most cases of ear disease.

The glands in the lining of the ear can excrete mineral salts and other toxins if these build up to an excessive amount in the body. If too much toxic material is excreted, the microclimate inside the ear changes, and this in turn will allow parasites and other micro-organisms to colonize the ear. The overgrowth of disease-causing organisms then produces an abnormal discharge.

A healthy ear, of whatever shape or size, will have a pale pink colour to the lining and a clean, healthy smell. The proprietary Indian herbal cream *Canador* is useful when there are mild disturbances. *Echinacea 6X*, or a herbal infusion, can be used to aid ear detoxification. Other non-specific ear cleaners are homeopathic and herbal preparations, such as *Hypercal* tincture (an equal mixture of *Hypericum* and *Calendula*) diluted 1:10 in water, two drops of lemon juice in 5ml (1 tsp) of almond oil, or three parts of *Rosemary* infusion with one part

witch hazel lotion. If the dog's constitutional homeopathic remedy is known, it will help to correct the underlying disorder.

The presence of dark, dry, crumbly wax in the ear often indicates the presence of canker mites. If these are suspected use one part each of *Rosemary*, *Rue* and *Thyme* infusion mixed with three parts of olive oil to clean the ear.

In any case, if the ears are very sore or if there is a profuse discharge, consult your vet, and support his conventional treatment with an appropriate remedy. Alternative treatments include the use of homeopathic *Graphites 6C* four times daily if the discharge is very sticky (similar to glue ear in children), *Hepar sulph. 30C* every two hours if the ear is very painful and sensitive. At a deeper level of treatment *Sulphur 30C* often helps dogs that are itchy and like to be cool, while *Psorinum 30C* is useful for itchy dogs that like to be warm. Dogs that need either of the last two remedies tend to be scruffy, dirty-looking animals.

rosemary

△ Rosemary has been prized since ancient times for its antiseptic properties. Used as an infusion, it can help clear the ear of mites.

aural haematoma

A dog's ear flap is essentially a bag of skin attached to an inner sheet of cartilage. The blood vessels that serve the ear lie on the inner side of the cartilage. If these vessels bleed, the blood fills and distends the bag in a condition known as aural haematoma, the same as happens in humans when boxers get cauliflower ears. This type of bleeding results from blows to the dog's ear or from a malfunction of the immune system.

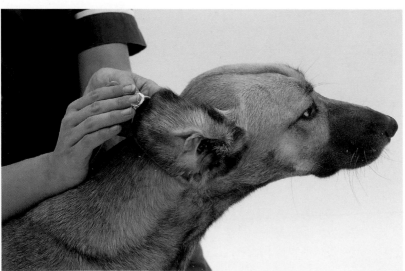

◁ Check the ears daily for abnormal smells and discharges. In summer, check also for the presence of grass awns. Applying the homeopathic pulsatilla cream will help alleviate irritations and minor sores in the ears.

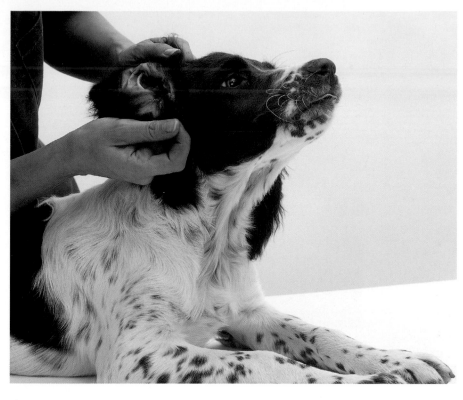

◁ The hair growing in the ear canal should be gently plucked, and excess hair removed from the inner surface of the ear to allow good ventilation.

Conventional veterinary treatment for aural haematoma involves cutting the inner surface of the ear to release the build up of blood, then sewing the two surfaces together like a mattress. This stops it refilling while the cut heals. Alternatively, the blood is drained using a wide-bore needle and a small dose of steroid injected into the ear using the same needle.

If the condition is caught in the very early stages, homeopathic *Arnica 6C* four times a day for two days, then *Hamamelis 12C* twice daily may reverse the process. *Hamamelis* cream or lotion can be applied to the ear flap. *Pulsatilla 6C* can be used instead of *Hamamelis* in gentle, affectionate dogs, and *Phosphorus 6C* often works in dogs that are sensitive to thunder. The tissue salt *Ferrum phos.* can be used if there is a tendency for the condition to recur.

middle and inner ear infections

Severe or neglected ear infections can spread to the middle and inner ear causing a head-tilt towards the affected side or a complete loss of balance. At this stage the

dog should certainly be taken to the vet. Dogs with recurrent ear infections should be referred to a holistic vet who will treat the underlying causes and will prescribe holistic support for any antibiotics given by the conventional vet. He will also treat any mineral imbalances or stress factors that may be involved. The dog's own homeopathic constitutional remedy can be supported by aromatherapy or a Bach Flower remedy at this time if stress factors are involved.

◁ The aromatherapy oil Roman chamomile, used in a burner, will soothe a dog who is suffering stress as an unseen cause of infection.

◁ Lemon juice has anti-inflammatory properties and can be used, when diluted with spring water, to clean healthy ears.

holistic dog care

Nasal discharges are uncommon in dogs. They do occur, however, in canine distemper, a viral disease which is potentially fatal. If the dog is also coughing, vomiting and suffering from diarrhoea, it should be seen by a vet as soon as possible. (Canine distemper will be discussed more fully under the nervous system.)

Sometimes nasal discharges can be the result of a foreign body, such as a grass awn, getting stuck in the nose. Generally, these foreign bodies need to be removed under a general anaesthetic, but try homeopathic *Silicia 200C* twice daily for five days. This may help to loosen the obstruction so that it comes out naturally.

Discharges can also result from fungal infections and tumours. A vet will need to carry out X-rays and blood tests to identify which is involved. Conventional treatment can be supported with a herbal infusion of *Golden Seal*, which reduces mucoid discharges, or homeopathic remedies: *Allium cepa 6C* four times a day if the discharge is thin and burns the nose, *Pulsatilla 6C* four times a day if it is bland and creamy and *Hydrastis 6C* four times a day if it is thick and white. If the X-rays show signs of bone destruction you can try *Acid nit.* if there is no smell, or *Aurum* if the discharge

◁ The dog's nose is as important as our eyes are to us. All discharges are therefore of great significance.

is foul smelling, both at the *6C* potency, four times a day. Herbal *Garlic* infusions or tablets benefit the immune system and help to fight infections, but they can interfere with the action of homeopathic remedies.

Nose bleeds can occur for a variety of reasons. They can follow blows, be caused by ulceration of the lining of the nose during infections, or be present where there are tumours or more serious diseases. Persistent or recurrent nose bleeds should always be checked by a vet. One-off cases can be treated by finger pressure on the nose, if the

dog will allow it. Otherwise, homeopathic remedies can be tried as follows: *Aconite 30C* every five minutes until the blood thickens and the flow slows down; if caused by a blow, *Arnica 6C* every 15 minutes reducing the dosage as the flow slows down; *Phosphorus 6C* every 15 minutes in active dogs which seek heat and fear thunder; and *Mellilotus 6C* every ten minutes if the bleeding is bright and flowing. The tissue salt *Ferrum phos.* will stop bleeding if sprinkled on to a wound; given twice daily it can help prevent the recurrence of bleeding.

◁ Homeopathic aconite given in a low potency every five minutes can help to thicken the blood and slow a nose bleed.

▷ A damp towel will help to stop the flow of blood if your dog has a nose bleed.

Physical problems: the throat and neck

Inflammation of the tonsils, other glands in the throat and of the larynx can result in coughs. If the cough is mild, there is no reason why home treatments cannot be tried. Homeopathic remedies include: *Calc. carb. 6C* four times a day in heavy, sluggish dogs with glandular enlargement; *Phytolacca 6C* four times a day where the throat looks a bluish/purple colour; or *Rhus tox. 6C* if the throat is an angry red colour and the glands are swollen. The tissue salt *Silicia* helps glandular function generally and is useful in chronic troubles. A herbal infusion of *Sage*, *Thyme* and *Liquorice* is also beneficial for coughs and glands.

Coughs that start after the dog has been exposed to dry, cold winds (typically the bitter, easterly winter winds) respond well to *Aconite*, while coughs that begin after exposure to damp, cold air in the evening following a mild day (as often occurs in autumn and winter for example) respond well to *Dulcamara*. Use the *6C* potency four times a day.

△ Coughs and colds caused by infections respond well to homeopathic remedies.

kennel cough

This is a bacterial or viral infection. The main organism responsible is usually related to the one responsible for whooping cough in humans. The cough is a harsh, dry, booming one and tends to be worse at night. The dog can be made to cough by gently putting pressure on its windpipe and larynx. It is often seen in dogs that have been away from home at kennels. The incubation period is about ten days, so it

walnuts

△ Heather, honeysuckle and walnut make a suitable combination for treating kennel cough.

▷ Coughs and colds with underlying emotional causes may need the help of a Flower Remedy.

often appears just after the dog comes home. Conventional veterinary treatment usually involves an antibiotic.

Because of the kennelling aspect it is likely that there are emotional factors involved in the disease, and so support with the Bach Flower remedies can be tried: *Heather* for loneliness; *Honeysuckle* for homesickness; and *Walnut* for difficulty in adapting to new circumstances. Of the homeopathic remedies, *Arsen. alb. 6C* can help dogs whose cough is worse in the early part of the night and *Drosera 6C* for those who are worse around 3 a.m. Give both remedies four times a day.

◁ Splinters from sticks picked up outdoors can easily become lodged in the back of the throat, causing tonsillitis and coughs.

Physical problems: the chest

The chest contains two major organs: the lungs and the heart. Disease of either of these can result in coughing. Persistent coughs should always be checked by a vet.

lungs

Inflammation of the lungs may start in the airways – bronchitis – and spread to the lung tissue itself – pneumonia. It is normally caused by a bacterial or viral infection, but can also be due to a tumour. If there is not a quick response to either conventional or complementary treatment, X-rays are essential. Conventional treatment is by antibiotics, often with steroids to suppress the inflammation. Short courses of steroid treatment are acceptable, but if long courses are prescribed, seek a holistic referral.

In mild cases inhalations of aromatic oils can provide useful support: *Eucalyptus* if there is a lot of mucus on the chest, and *Tea Tree* or *Thyme* where infections are suspected. Homeopathic *Aconite 6C* can be given in frequent doses if you catch the cough at the early stage where the temperature is starting to rise. Follow this with *Belladonna 6C* also given in frequent doses as the fever peaks. Once the initial stages have passed, give support with one of the following remedies: *Bryonia 6C* if the dog

◁ **Dandelion is a diuretic. Herbal infusions can reduce the build up of fluid in the lungs in the first stage of heart disease.**

dandelion leaf

▷ **Infusions and tablets of garlic are widely used for asthma and bronchitis because of anti-bacterial properties. However, garlic may suppress homeopathic remedies.**

garlic cloves

resents moving, does not want to be touched and drinks a lot at long intervals; *Phosphorus* if there is blood in the sputum; *Kali carb.* if the cough is at its worst about 3 a.m.; *Rumex crisp* if the cough is worse by day; *Spongia* if the cough is at its worse at night and *Antimon. tart.* if the respiration sounds rattling. Give these four times daily.

Tissue salts can also help. Give *Ferrum phos.* for harsh, dry coughs, *Kali sulph.* when yellow phlegm is coughed up, and *Kali mur.* for white phlegm.

Herbal infusions of *Mullein* are good for night-time coughs; *Thyme* and *Liquorice* help coughs generally. *Garlic* helps the immune system fight infections, but it may act as an unwitting antidote to homeopathic remedies.

◁ **Coughs may be caused by heart problems as well as lung infections. Persistent coughing that does not show signs of abating should always be checked by a vet.**

◁ **Symptoms of heart disfunction include the dog's unwillingness to exercise and a soft dry cough when it does.**

heart

Heart-coughs are usually dry and brought on by exercise. As the heart function deteriorates, body fluids seep into the body tissues, where they cause swellings or oedema, and into the body cavities where they cause dropsy. As the lungs fill with fluid, the cough worsens becoming soft and moist. Dropsy can also result from liver troubles and tumours, so it is worth having the dog checked if symptoms appear.

Conventional veterinary treatment for heart-coughs is to use diuretics, to remove water from the body, and circulatory stimulants. Complementary remedies can be very successful and could mean that conventional treatment can be delayed or reduced.

Ask yourself first if there may be any underlying emotional cause to the cough: think along the lines of a broken heart. If so, the Bach Flower remedies *Heather* for loneliness, *Star of Bethlehem* for emotional shock and *Walnut* for difficulty in coping with change can be considered.

Homeopathic low-potency herbals are effective in well-chosen cases, but these

have to be prescribed by a homeopathic vet for accuracy. As well as treating the cough, the vet may also prescribe a constitutional prescription which will help treat the underlying causes. Remedies that help are *Spongia 6C* for coughs worse at night and *Rumex 6C* if it is worse by day. Give them four times a day. Sometimes these are more effective when given in higher potencies, but the vet would advise on this. *Digitalis 30C* helps when the pulse is very slow and *Carbo veg. 30C* when there is a great desire for fresh air as well as a slow pulse. Give these twice daily. *Cactus grandiflora 6C* can be given up to four times daily if there appears to be a great deal of pain in the chest.

If swellings develop in the limbs *Apis mell. 6C* four times a day can help. If the dog is restless and its cough is worse around midnight try *Arsenicum*, but if the cough is at its worse around 4 a.m. and 4 p.m. try *Lycopodium*. The tissue salts *Calc. fluor.* given twice daily can help to strengthen the heart muscles and *Kali phos.* can help if the dog's heartbeat is abnormal. Herbal infusions of either *Dandelion* or *Hawthorn* can also help.

Dietary advice is to give the dog a low-salt diet: proprietary heart diets are lower in salt than normal ones. Conventional diuretics can result in the loss of phosphorus from the body: if your vet recommends a phosphorus supplement try seaweed powder, which is rich in minerals and vitamins, or the tissue salt *Kali phos.* Reduce exercise to a steady level to avoid undue distress.

eucalyptus

△ **Eucalyptus oil has antiseptic and expectorant properties, and works well for dogs in a diffuser.**

Physical problems: the abdomen

The abdomen contains the stomach, intestines, liver, pancreas, kidneys, bladder and the sex organs – the ovaries and uterus of the female and the prostate of the male.

Disease of these organs is accompanied by severe pains and can cause vomiting and/or diarrhoea. If the pain is behind the ribs it is probably related to a liver problem. Pain in the triangle between the ribs and the back muscles can relate to the kidneys or ovaries. General abdominal pains indicate intestinal trouble, and pain in the rear abdomen points to the bladder or prostate.

vomiting and/or diarrhoea

These may be the result of a either a primary or a secondary stomach inflammation. A primary inflammation can be caused by food and other poisoning, eating too much rich food, and swallowing foreign bodies – such as stones and children's toys – but is rarely due to tumours. A secondary inflammation results from a primary and more serious disease in the liver, kidney or pancreas. If blood is present or if symptoms persist for more than 24 hours you should see the vet. He may wish to X-ray for foreign bodies, especially if there is vomiting first thing in the morning, or take blood samples to look for underlying causes.

In all cases treatment will either be by antibiotics for infections, anti-inflammatory steroids to control inflammation, anabolic steroids when there is loss of body weight, insulin when diabetes is present and fluid replacement if there is concern about dehydration. Dietary changes, such as vitamin and mineral supplements, and medical diets may also be suggested.

Complementary support does help acute conditions, and can reduce dose levels in chronic cases. An immediate first aid step is to stop feeding the dog and to give a little salt if it is vomiting, or bicarbonate of soda if it has diarrhoea. If stress is implicated try the Bach Flowers: *Aspen* for fear, *Chicory* for separation anxiety and attention seeking, and *Impatiens* for the irritability associated with Irritable Bowel Syndrome. *Rescue Remedy* may help severe pains and ease the dog's distress.

Of the homeopathic remedies used for vomiting and diarrhoea, *Arsen. alb.* helps if the dog is restless and gets worse around midnight, and thirsts for a little water very often. *Phosphorus* can be tried if the dog is very thirsty for large quantities, yet vomits 15–20 minutes after drinking; blood may be present. *Ipecacuana* is for persistent vomiting and diarrhoea, often with bloody mucus, this may follow eating indigestible food. Alternatively, try *Nux vom.* for vomiting after rich food, *Aloes* for diarrhoea with flatulence, *Podophyllum* for watery stools, *Chamomilla* for teething pups if the stools are green and *Capsicum* for light-coloured recurrent diarrhoea in rehomed pups. In all cases give the *6C* potency frequently, reducing the time between doses as the condition improves.

△ **Rosemary oil vapour is inhaled for its anti-inflammatory properties. Use with mint to ease acute liver problems, and with wild marjoram for chronic ones.**

Herbal infusions of *Gentian*, *St John's Wort* and *Peppermint* ease the stomach while *Slippery Elm* and *Arrowroot* help to soothe the intestines.

Tissue salts can help. If the dog is vomiting undigested food, try *Ferrum phos*; *Kali mur.* for thick mucus, *Nat phos.* for sour, acid vomit and *Natrum sulph.* for yellowy green bile. For diarrhoea from anxiety use *Kali phos.*, or *Natrum mur.* if it alternates with constipation. As the dog improves, slowly reintroduce a bland diet, such as fish or chicken (off the bone) with rice or pasta.

Bloating is a distension of the abdomen with gas, caused by excessive fermentation

◁ **Children's toys hold a fascination for dogs, who can easily swallow them, often with disastrous results.**

of the stomach contents, and is very painful. If the dog can pass wind or belch, *Carbo veg. 6C* every 15 minutes helps. However, if the dog is doubled-up in pain, this is an emergency and you must call the vet at once. While you are waiting, use *Colchicum* if the dog lies still and *Colocynth* if it rolls in agony.

liver and kidneys

Liver disease causes the vomiting of bile, pain behind the ribs, loss of appetite and eventually jaundice. Kidney problems may be indicated either by thirstlessness or an extreme thirst with vomiting. Chronic kidney problems lead to increased urination, loss of appetite, high thirst and vomiting, weight-loss and dehydration.

For severe liver and kidney trouble, the Bach Flower *Crab Apple* helps to detoxify the body. Homeopathic *Lycopodium* helps liver symptoms that worsen around 4 p.m., *Chelidonium* for early jaundice with vomiting and/or diarrhoea and *Carduus marianus* for dropsy, jaundice and hard, dry stools.

Kidney problems with intense thirst, weight loss and greasy hair respond to homeopathic *Natrum mur. Merc. sol.* helps if there is a lot of saliva present and ulcers start to form in the mouth, and *Kali chlor.* if the breath is putrid and the ulcers greyish.

Herbal infusions of *Dandelion* helps the liver, *Bearberry* helps the kidneys and *Barberry* helps both liver and kidney problems. The aromatic oil of *Rosemary* can help liver problems while *Juniper* helps those of the kidney and bladder.

pancreas

Both acute and chronic conditions of the pancreas should be diagnosed by a vet. Homeopathic *Iris ver.* is useful if the dog is restless and vomits mainly at night. The tissue salts *Natrum phos.* and *Ferrum phos.* can help with acute problems, as can herbal infusions of *Gentian*.

bladder

Bladder problems can be due to infections or to the sedimentation of crystals and stones in the urine. These may arise through kidney problems, or because the dog is not

tarragon

◁ **Tarragon oil has an antispasmodic and calming action when used by inhalation.**

holistic dog care

drinking enough water, or because its urine is too alkaline. Crystals can lump together to form stones. Both crystals and stones can cause mechanical obstructions. Signs of bladder problems are frequent attempts to urinate, straining to urinate, blood-stained urine, or the involuntary passing of urine. In most cases, abdominal pain will be present and you should see the vet.

Complementary therapies will help, particularly in chronic disorders. Sudden onset of straining to pass small amounts of bloody urine often responds to twice-hourly homeopathic *Cantharis 6C* or *Merc. sol. 6C* if there is a lot of mucus present as well. *Causticum 6C* twice daily is helpful in chronic, recurrent cases. If the vet says there are a lot of crystals present, *Thlaspi bursa 6C* can be very helpful. *Equisetum*, which is both a herbal and a homeopathic remedy, can help frequency when large amounts of urine are passed painfully a few drops at a time. Herbal infusions of *Buchu* can help to dissolve any gravel-like deposits that may be present in the bladder.

Incontinence in dogs can be treated with homeopathic *Causticum* in elderly, warty dogs and *Staphysagria* in recently kennelled ones. The Bach Flower remedies *Aspen* for emotional stress and *Olive* for emotional weakness can also help.

◁ **The Bach Flower remedies are useful in stress-related bowel problems in dogs.**

Physical problems: the skin

The skin is the largest organ of the body. It protects against the elements, helps to control body temperature, and excretes waste via sweat and sebum produced in the sebaceous glands. The skin is the body's barrier against the outside world, and it is on the skin that many underlying problems will first be seen.

In disease, body metabolism is disturbed and this results in abnormal secretions from the sebaceous glands, which change the skin's microclimate and lead to the development of skin infections or skin disease. Conventional treatment is excellent at reducing pain and inflammation in acute conditions, but it is not able to remedy the underlying defect in metabolism.

Prolonged or frequently repeated skin treatment leads to suppression of symptoms, which in turn can lead to the establishment of chronic and sometimes drug-induced disease. Chronic skin diseases are based upon

malnutrition, hormonal imbalances and emotional problems that stress the immune system, opening the way for bacterial and fungal infections and parasitic infestations. All chronic skin problems will benefit from the support of holistic treatment no matter what their conventional categorization.

parasitic skin disease

External parasites include fleas, lice, ticks, harvest mites and Cheyletiella mites. Fleas are reddish brown in colour and move quickly; lice are grey, slow-moving and are often found on the ears; ticks look like warts and are removed using special hooks available from your vet. Harvest mites are orange or red and are found between the toes; Cheyletiella are whitish in colour, slow-moving and are known as walking dandruff.

Conventional treatment for external parasites involves strong chemicals to kill

◁ The evergreen citrus tree neroli is native to China. Its floral essential oil works well for anxiety- and stress-related skin conditions.

neroli

the insects. Complementary treatments repel the insects rather than kill them. A herbal treatment, *Xenex*, has been shown to repel fleas for up to 40 days. Herbal *Garlic* will repel them, as will homeopathic *Sulphur* given weekly, or three drops of one of the essential oils of *Cedarwood*, *Eucalyptus*, *Lavender*, *Lemon*, *Mint*, *Rosemary* or *Terebinth* added to 150ml (¼ pint) of water and brushed into the coat.

Two species of mite live on the skin. The Sarcoptic mite affects humans and dogs, and causes red spots that itch uncontrollably in both species. The Demodex mite is only a problem if there is a defect in the immune system. First signs may be a spectacle-like balding, which starts around the eyes and spreads over the body. Strong conventional washes are needed to kill both mites.

As complementary support therapies, homeopathic *Sulphur* can help dogs that dislike being warm, and *Psorinum* those who want to be as warm as possible. *Garlic* tablets help, but they may interfere with homeopathic treatments. The tissue salt *Calc. sulph.* is beneficial, but not a complete cure, while essential oil of *Lavender*, *Lemon* or *Wild Marjoram* can be used in diluted form in the same way as for parasites.

eczema and dermatitis

These conditions need a holistic consultation to get a cure. If stress is implicated the Bach Flowers are helpful: *Agrimony* helps skin irritation due to anxiety, *Crab Apple*

◁ A daily spoonful of fish oils makes a tasty treat, and the extra minerals it adds to the diet will help soothe dry and inflamed skins.

▷ Do not forget to check the underneath of your dog. Many conditions first appear in the armpit and groin areas.

if the dog is toxic, the skin is dirty-looking, the hair is matted and secondary skin infections are present. *Holly* aids allergic conditions, especially in malicious dogs. Aromatherapy using *Rosemary* and *Lavender*, or *Lavender*, *Pine* and *Terebinth* to massage unaffected areas of the body does help. Homeopathic treatments include *Hypercal* tincture diluted 1:10 to cleanse the skin, tablets of *Sulphur* if the skin is hot, dry and itchy and the dog dislikes heat, and *Psorinum* for dirty-looking, itchy, smelly dogs that want to be warm. Use *Apis mel.* for allergies where the skin is shiny, red, dry, and better if cold, or *Urtica* if these symptoms are eased by warmth. *Lycopodium* is useful where

there is an underlying liver problem and *Natrum mur.* if there is long-standing grief. In acute cases use *6C* potency several times a day; in chronic cases use *30C* potency twice daily. Herbal infusions of *Oak bark* or a decoction of *Mallow* can be used as compresses, and *Aloe Vera* gel is useful on dry inflamed skins. Nutritional support with *Evening Primrose* and fish oils will help in long-standing cases.

hair loss

If this is the result of skin disease it is treated as above. If it is bilaterally symmetrical there may be an underlying hormonal imbalance. The Bach Flower *Scleranthus* helps to restore balance. One of the following combinations of essential oils is helpful in massage: *Calamus* and *Lavender*; *Pine* and *Terebinth*; *Cedar* and *Thyme*. Homeopathic *Sepia* or *Pulsatilla* will balance a bitch's hormones

if the animal's constitution matches the remedy; *Lycopodium* can help old, lean dogs that are prematurely grey if they loose their hair, and *Thallium* is good for general hair growth. Use the *30C* potency weekly until signs of regrowth are seen.

warts

These are common in old age and are difficult to treat by any therapy. Surgery is best avoided unless the warts are causing trouble. Homeopathic *Thuja* tincture can be painted on the wart twice daily for up to three months, *Causticum 6C* twice daily helps old, stiff dogs with warts and *Nitric acid 6C* twice daily helps if the warts are close to the eyes, ears, mouth or anus. A piece of banana skin taped over the wart and replaced fresh each day has been known to work, as have the tissue salts *Kali mur.* and *Natrum mur.*

△ Dogs may develop allergies to parasites which will require conventional care to alleviate the problem quickly. Alternative therapies can be used in a supporting role.

▷ When massaging oils remember that they must be well diluted with a suitable carrier oil, and that dogs are more sensitive than humans to their toxic effects.

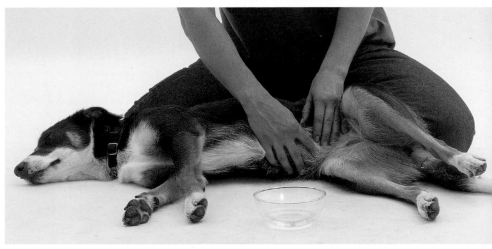

The ovaries and uterus are the organs responsible for reproduction in the female. The ovaries do not normally cause primary trouble. Cystic ovaries lead to hormonal imbalances, but the symptoms are produced elsewhere in the body. Serious problems may occur, however, in the uterus.

The uterus may become infected following an abortion or after giving birth (metritis) and can usually be treated by antibiotics. Sometimes the contents of the uterus build up and distend it (pyometritis); this is often a sequel to recurrent false pregnancies or repeated contraceptive treatments. If the cervix is open, profuse discharges occur, and if it remains closed, pressure in the uterus causes pain and collapse. In both cases a toxaemia occurs that can be fatal. Pyometritis usually needs an emergency ovario-hysterectomy.

Complementary care may eliminate the need for surgery if the condition is caught early enough. Homeopathic remedies using *30C* potencies up to four times a day are beneficial. Use *Sepia* if the bitch is dull and irritable, has a high thirst and a brownish discharge; *Caulophyllum* if the discharge is chocolate brown in colour; *Hydrastis* if the discharge is white mucus, but use *Pulsatilla* in the more unusual case where the thirst is low and the discharge creamy yellow. If the discharge is bloody, use *Sabina*. Herbal *Golden Seal* can help catarrhal discharges and *Myrrh* foul ones.

△ Inhalation of lavender oil will help relax a bitch who is stressed by hormonal imbalance. Give her only a momentary sniff of the bottle: the canine sense of smell is extremely keen.

miscarriages

Bitches may fail to carry pups to full-term due to infections, hormonal imbalances or poor nutrition. Early abortions may result only in a catarrhal vaginal discharge, in late pregnancy dead foetuses are expelled along with some pus. Discharges should be treated as for metritis. Bitches with a tendency to abort repeatedly can be given homeopathic *Viburnum opulis 30C* weekly for the first month of pregnancy and *Caulophyllum* weekly for the last five weeks. The tissue salt *Calc. phos.* helps to maintain a healthy uterus during pregnancy.

false pregnancy

Bitches may act as if they are pregnant, nest and come into milk after a season even though they have not been mated. In the wild, bitches may be needed to act as foster mothers to abandoned or orphaned pups, but in the family setting the behavioural changes that accompany false pregnancies can be distressing. Homeopathic treatment is much more successful than conventional in this case. *Sepia* aids grumpy bitches with high thirsts, while *Pulsatilla* will help the affectionate thirstless ones and *Clematis* those whose milk is dropping from them. Use a *30C* tablet up to four times a day.

◁ Infusions of golden seal or myrrh have been found to be useful in early cases of pyrometritis.

▽ Scleranthus can restore stability to bitches with any type of hormonal imbalance.

sage

◁ Sage helps if there is pain when the bitch is in heat, if given as an infusion.

The reproductive system of the male is far simpler than that of the bitch. Its function is constant, not cyclic, and there is less that can go wrong.

the penis

This is not usually affected other than by trauma following the misjudgement of a jump. Treatment should be according to the injury. However, the penis is very vascular: cuts can bleed for some time and often need to be stitched.

the prostate gland

This is a small gland that surrounds the first part of the urethra, and lies just in front of the pelvic brim. Normally it cannot be felt, but if it enlarges due to infection or tumours, or in old age, it can be felt by a vet during an internal examination. When enlarged, the prostate puts pressure on the urethra, restricting the flow of urine and causing pain, and blood will appear in the urine. If the prostate swells enough it can move backwards into the pelvis where it acts as a blockage, restricting the passage of faeces. The dog then produces thin watery stools which bypass the obstruction. There is an apparent constipation as stools do not pass the obstruction, but the pain will cause the dog to walk with its back arched and as if it were knock-kneed. Conventional treatment with anti-male hormones shrinks the prostate to its normal size. If it becomes a recurrent problem, castration is advised. This removes the source of male hormones and the prostate withers away.

Complementary medicine is effective. The Bach Flower *Scleranthus* can help to restore balance to the hormone system. Homeopathic remedies also help. *Sabal serrulata 3X*, three drops given three times a day, acts directly on the prostate in the majority of dogs. *Pulsatilla 30C* twice daily is helpful in affectionate but jealous dogs;

clematis

△ Puppies may experience difficulty in urination due to juvenile hormone problems. Homeopathic Clematis will help relieve the problem.

Ipecacuana 6C given hourly will stop profuse bleeding due to ulceration of the urethra; *Clematis 6C* given four times daily aids young dogs with upset hormones; *Agnus castus* helps old dogs with shrivelled testes, and *Digitalis 6C* given every two hours helps if the problem is sudden and painful. The tissue salt *Silicia* can help the older dog with prostate troubles.

the testicles

These sperm-producing organs rarely cause disease. The main problem associated with the testicles is tumours in old age. These are best treated by surgical removal. Castration is also recommended for hypersexuality, but it only works effectively if there is an overactive prostate gland.

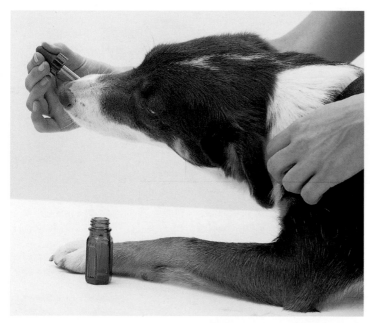

◁ Sabal serrulata is more helpful in the case of senile prostatic hypertrophy. It is used as a low potency liquid.

holistic dog care

The endocrine glands produce hormones that are carried around the body in the blood to other organs and tissues whose function they help to control.

There are three endocrine glands, the pituitary, adrenal and ovaries, and between them they control the female reproductive cycle and pregnancy. The thyroid controls the body's metabolic rate, and the pancreas controls the glucose metabolism. The adrenal gland produces cortisone and other steroids which control many functions.

An over-production of cortisone, or Cushing's disease, may be due to tumours of the pituitary gland or of the adrenal gland itself. An underproduction of cortisone, or Addison's disease, can result from the gland's capacity being suppressed by prolonged use or over-dosage of cortisone-type drugs, or tumours of the adrenal gland.

All these diseases will lead to weakness and lethargy. A high thirst is common to diabetes, Cushing's and Addison's disease, and hair loss is seen in hypothyroidism and Cushing's. If your dog shows symptoms of any one of these diseases you must see your vet immediately. He will make a diagnosis based on blood and urine tests, and will prescribe a course of treatment.

parsley

In general, hormone deficiencies are best treated by conventional replacement therapy, such as insulin for diabetes, or thyroid extract for hypothyroidism. Holistic treatment can help to reduce the amount required and give a better quality of life. If alternative support is given, the hormone levels should be carefully monitored by the vet so that drug overdoses are not given.

The Bach Flower *Scleranthus* will help stabilize any endocrine organ. Homeopathic preparations made from normal glands (sarcodes) can help if given in the *30C* potency, weekly; *Pancreatinum* for diabetes, *Thyroidinum* for hypothyroidism, *Cortisone 30C* for the adrenal gland and *Pituitrin* if the pituitary

◁ The diuretic effect of a parsley infusion can help to control the dropsy seen in both Cushing's and Addison's disease.

▽ Haricot beans mixed into the dog's food will have a beneficial effect on the pancreas and can be used in both acute and chronic pancreatitis.

haricot beans

gland is involved. In addition, *Iris ver.* will aid the pancreas generally. *Syzygium 6C* will stimulate the body's natural insulin production, while *Thyroidinum 6X* acts as a replacement for thyroid extract. *Natrum mur.* as a tissue salt can help any type of hormonal problem, and in homeopathic form can be used as a constitutional remedy. Herbal *Seaweed* tablets and *Garlic* are used for hypothyroidism, and *Dandelion*, *Nettle* and *Parsley* infusion for adrenal problems.

◁ Homeopathic sarcodes help restore function to endocrine glands for a return to health. Use only with veterinary supervision.

Physical problems: the nervous system

This consists of the brain, spinal cord and peripheral nerves. Physical trauma to the spine can injure the spinal cord causing paralysis, but this will be considered under the locomotor system.

Convulsions, or fits, can result from viral infections such as canine distemper, metabolic diseases such as diabetes and milk fever, poisons – particularly lead, slug-bait and anti-freeze – and tumours of the brain. Sometimes no known cause is found. Fits are not painful to the dog. It should be left in a quiet, dark, cool place to come round before it is taken to the vet unless the fits become continuous. This is an emergency and the dog should be seen at once.

Inflammation of the nerves is known as neuritis. It is extremely painful and may result from mechanical injury to the nerve or pressure on it from a tumour or other swelling. Inflammation of the brain itself is called encephalitis while meningitis is inflammation of the surrounding brain membranes. Both of these can be caused by bacterial and viral infections and tumours. The symptoms can be behavioural changes, head pressing, swaying, falling and severe convulsions. Chorea is uncontrollable

◁ Distemper is the most common cause of fits and chorea. Vaccination does give protection but does have more side effects than is often recognized. If side effects are suspected, complementary treatment is essential.

twitching. It is usually a long-term effect of canine distemper but poisons and brain tumours can also be to blame.

Conventional treatment for all these conditions is based on anti-convulsants plus antibiotics if bacterial infections are suspected. Complementary support is very valuable. The Bach Flowers can be used: *Crab Apple* helps in any case of poisoning;

◁ Neuralgias respond very well to homeopathic chamomile if given every fifteen minutes. It is particularly useful for teething pains.

Holly can restore balance if the onset of symptoms is very quick; and *Cherry Plum* calms uncontrollable behaviour and fits. The homeopathic remedy *Belladonna* is good for dogs whose pupils remain widely dilated after fits, *Strammonium* for dogs which stagger just before the start of a fit and fall to the left. *Cocculus 6C* given daily for one month then in the *30C* potency weekly for three months may prevent the recurrence of fits. *Agaricus* helps twitching associated with convulsions and *Cuprum* or *Zinc* for twitching only. Give both remedies as a *6C* twice daily. Aromatic oil of *Lavender* by diffuser calms and sedates the nervous system, as do herbal infusions of *Skullcap* and *Valerian*.

Nerve pain resulting from a heavy blow will respond to homeopathic *Hypericum*, *Chamomilla* helps if the pain makes the dog snappy, while *Spigelia* helps facial neuralgia, *Colocynth* left-sided neuralgia and *Mag. phos.* right-sided pains. Herbal infusions of *Oats* or *Passiflora* also help neuralgias.

◁ Lavender oil calms and sedates the nervous system and can be used as an inhalation in all nerve conditions.

Physical problems: the locomotor system

The locomotor system consists of the muscles, bones and joints of the body, and disease is usually accompanied by pain.

Severe, sudden-onset pain is normally caused by accidents and acute infections; chronic low-grade pain is usually due to rheumatism (muscle-based) or arthritis (bony changes in the joints). All dogs involved in accidents that cause great pain, lameness, or unconciousness should be seen as quickly as possible by a vet. Low-grade stiffness that lasts for more than five days should also be checked so that X-rays can be taken. Fractures and dislocations will need surgical treatment. Antibiotics are usually given if infection is suspected. Pain relief is normally with non-steroidal anti-inflammatory drugs, but steroids may be used for serious back pains.

Severe back pain can arise from partial dislocation or misalignment of the veterbrae, intervertebral disc disease and arthritis of the intervertebral joints (spondylitis). Two other painful conditions are inflammation of muscles (myositis) and inflammation of bone (osteitis). Both are due to infection or bruising. There are also developmental diseases which occur in dogs. Hip dysplasia, in which the hip joint fails to develop normally, results in early chronic arthritis. There is also osteochondritis dessicans (OCD) in which the cartilaginous surfaces in the joints of large-breed dogs degenerates between six and 12 months of age.

All these conditions are extremely suitable for complementary treatment or support. The Bach Flower *Rescue Remedy* or homeopathic *Aconite 6C* should be given as soon as possible after any accident. These can be followed by homeopathic *Arnica 6C* as often as needed. If there is no fracture or dislocation, back pain can be treated by acupuncture, chiropractic or osteopathy. Limb pains can be treated by one of the massage therapies already mentioned. Aromatherapy massage with *Rosemary* or *Birch* oils can also help. Where there is no major injury but the dog is reluctant to use its leg, homeopathic *Bryonia* is used instead of *Arnica*; this is followed by *Ruta grav.* and finally *Rhus tox.* Use the *6C* potency four times a day for all remedies. If infection is present, *Hepar sulph. 30C* can be used for muscles and joints, but *Hepar sulph. 200C* may be tried if there is a bone infection. If it does not help, use *Calc. fluor. 6C* until the pus finds a way to the surface, then change to *Calc. sulph.*

All bone and joint surgery should be supported by *Arnica* at the time of the operation, and *Arnica* or *Bryonia* for 24 hours afterwards, the choice being made as above. Further support with weekly doses of homeopathic *Calc. phos. 30C* to balance calcium metabolism and *Symphytum 12C* to stimulate the cells that repair the bones can be given. If the dog is from a large breed *Calc. carb.* can be used instead of *Calc. phos.*

mallow

◁ Infusions of mallow will speed the healing of sprains and strains, especially if used in conjunction with a TTouch massage.

feverfew

▷ Feverfew's analgesic effects, widely used for human migraines, are also beneficial for muscle and joint pains.

rheumatism

Rheumatism can be helped a lot by acupuncture, physiotherapy and massage therapies. The Bach Flowers can also be helpful: *Beech* can help dogs that are rigid and stiff with pain, try *Impatiens* for those that become irritable, whilst *Rock Water* can restore physical flexibility to dogs that are mentally as well as physically worn and need a fixed routine. The homeopathic remedy *Rhus tox.* helps classical rheumatism, which is worse in cold, damp weather and is better for gentle exercise in restless dogs, *Causticum* helps the stiff, prematurely ageing, warty dog, *Caulophyllum* helps where the knee, hock and other small joints are involved and *Calc. fluor.* given weekly can help to dissolve bony changes. Dietary supplements of *Evening Primrose* and *Cod Liver Oil*, and *Royal Jelly* help, as do *Vitamins B, C* and *E*. *Chondroitin sulphate* and *Green-lipped Mussel* extract help where there are cartilaginous defects and changes. These supplements are also useful in OCD.

hip dysplasia

This condition can be helped but not cured. The same treatments for arthritis can be given with the same nutritional support

◁ 5ml (1 tsp) cider vinegar in 600ml (1 pint) drinking water, along with vitamin supplements and royal jelly, will help to keep muscle pains away.

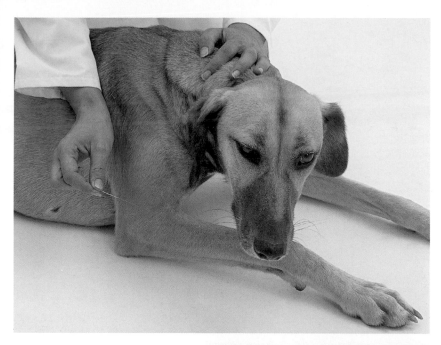

◁ Acupuncture is becoming
more popular as a treatment
for limb and back pain.

▽ Most dogs with strains and
pains will benefit from having
an intensely cold compress
pressed against the affected
limb. A suitable compress,
easily available at home,
would be a bag of frozen peas.

as for rheumatism. Dogs of breeds that are more susceptible to this condition should always be X-rayed before breeding. Vets will usually advise not to breed from dogs that show signs of the disease.

CDRM

German Shepherd dogs are affected by a disease in which they develop a degeneration of the nerve bundles in the spinal cord (CDRM). The nerves that tell the dog where its feet are in space are affected first. This results in a painless paralysis of the hind legs and the dog sways as it walks; it can look similar to hip dysplasia. This is incurable, and progresses slowly to stumbling on rough ground and dragging the top of the foot along the ground so that the nails are worn away. Healing massage therapies can help, while among the Bach Flowers *Crab Apple* helps if there are a lot of toxins in the dog's system and *Oak* helps stoical dogs that try to ignore their problem. In homeopathy *Conium maculatum* can delay progress but needs to be given in rising potencies as the case progresses, while *Plumbum,* for painless paralysis, is helpful if one side is more affected than the other. The tissue salt *Kali phos.* may be helpful to stimulate the nerves.

Physical problems: neoplasia

The literal meaning of neoplasia is new growths. The condition arises when cells in the body begin to multiply for no reason, causing tumours and cancers which may be either benign or malignant.

The term tumour is generally reserved for the benign neoplasms, and cancer for the malignant ones. A benign tumour does not spread to other parts of the body and usually has a clearly defined edge, whereas the malignant growth sends tentacles of abnormal cells into the surrounding tissues so that it is impossible to tell what is healthy and what is abnormal tissue. The malignant tumour also has a tendency to spread to other parts of the body by the blood or lymphatic system.

Tumours which are benign are generally non life-threatening, although a malignant but inactive growth can also be described as benign. On the other hand, a benign tumour, which has a defined shape and size and is not spreading to other parts of the body, may become life-threatening because of its size and/or because of the pressure it puts on a vital organ. This is what happens in the case of brain tumours, for example.

Neoplasm can include anything from harmless warts or papillomas at one end of the scale, to highly malignant cancers at the other that are capable of killing the patient in just a few weeks. Current medical science recognizes that neoplasms can develop after exposure to cancer-inducing agents (carcinogens), including some chemicals and tobacco, and to radiation from the sun and radioactive material. Neoplasms are also regarded as diseases in their own right.

treatment

Conventional veterinary treatment for malignant tumours focuses on fighting the cancer as vigorously as possible. Treatment is by sharp-knife surgery, laser surgery, chemotherapy and radiation therapy, or more likely than not, a combination of all of these techniques.

◁ Holistic treatment of neoplasms is more beneficial to the patient than conventional treatment alone.

From a holistic point-of-view, malignant neoplasms are viewed as an end-point of a disease process that may be of either long or short duration. The body is trying to store potentially toxic material that it cannot excrete by a normal route. These toxins are a result of the body's attempts to cope with the carcinogens. Its attempts may be adversely affected by stress factors, both physical and emotional. It is not known why the neoplasms develop in the first place: if it were purely a case of exposure to carcinogens, then everyone who smokes tobacco would develop cancer. Neoplasms develop when the patient does not recognize the importance of apparently minor symptoms; or when the patient's vitality is weak and he is unable to respond to therapy; or when the therapist fails to cure the early symptoms, allowing the neoplasm to manifest itself.

Good complementary therapy will prevent many diseases from developing to the cancer stage. Some veterinary practices have reported a marked diminution in the number of cancer cases after introducing holistic methods. Good holistic treatment can also reverse the very early stages, or can induce long-lasting remissions in cases that would otherwise progress to death.

Deciding which therapies should be used is a personal choice. The subject should be discussed thoroughly with your vet and with a therapist chosen by you and your vet. Go through all the options together. The best approach is to use a mixture of complementary and conventional methods. If the dog is too weak to undergo conventional treatment, complementary support will be helpful. Surgery should always be supported by trauma remedies. Dogs undergoing chemotherapy or radiotherapy can be given treatment to help reduce the side effects, and all cases should be given treatment to deal with the underlying causes once the active treatment is over.

There has been plenty of discussion as to what type of result can be claimed to be successful in terms of holistic therapy.

If the neoplasm disappears completely and does not return that is a success, as is a case where the growth stops and does not reappear. For many people, if holistic treatment can lead to a calm, painless and natural death, rather than necessitating more suffering followed by euthanasia, then it too has been successful. For some, a treatment that leads to a longer but more painful life is not beneficial to the dog.

The Bach Flower remedies *Agrimony, Gentian, Gorse, Impatiens, Mustard, Oak* and *Olive* have all been found to help in cancer cases: the choice of remedy should depend on the dog's mental state at any particular stage of the disease.

Reiki, TTouch massage and acupuncture can be beneficial in helping to relieve pain and bring calmness and balance to the dog. In a condition as serious as cancer, consult a professional therapist for advice.

Homeopathy is helpful both in supporting conventional treatment and afterwards, when trying to treat the underlying cause of the illness. At the time of surgery, *Arnica Hypericum* and *Calendula* will help to reduce bruising and pain and will help the skin to repair and heal. *Calc. phos.* and *Symphytum* can be given if bone surgery is needed. The side effects of chemotherapy can be alleviated by a skilled therapist, while *Uranium 30C* helps with radiation sickness and burns.

Non-specific support is given by *Viscum alb. Echinacea* will strengthen the immune system, and either *Hydrastis* or *Eupatorium perfoliatum* will help to relieve pains.

broccoli

aloe vera

beetroot (beets)

carrots

garlic cloves

royal jelly

Arsenicum alb., given in rising potencies, can remove the fear of dying from a terminally ill dog and will allow an easy transition from life to death. If the dog's own constitutional remedy can be found, remarkable results are possible, but a consultation of up to an hour may be needed to find it.

Anthroposophical preparations of mistletoe (*Viscum abnova* and *Iscador*) are widely used for human cancers and are now being requested for dogs by owners who have heard that humans respond well to it. The treatment is an injection given twice weekly, and only by the vet until the optimum dose is found. If you are interested in this treat-

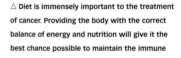
△ Diet is immensely important to the treatment of cancer. Providing the body with the correct balance of energy and nutrition will give it the best chance possible to maintain the immune

ment for your dog, discuss it with your vet. It will probably be a new approach for him and he may need to get more information before starting treatment.

Herbal infusions of *Red Clover*, a general anti-cancer agent, *Echinacea*, an immune system stimulant, and *Autumn Crocus,* for pain relief, are useful if given twice daily.

Support from the tissue salt *Calc. phos.* to stimulate the body's metabolism may help. Nutrition is also vital. Broccoli, beetroot (beets) and carrots are traditional anti-cancer vegetables, and can be added to the puréed portion of the Billinghurst diet. Supplements of Vitamins A, B complex, C and E can slow the growth rate of tumours. Royal jelly, aloe vera and garlic are helpful in a non-specific way.

Holistic treatment does not claim to cure all cancers because in most cases cancer is still a terminal disease. However, holistic care will reduce pain and suffering (both emotional and physical), and it will prolong the period of happy life. It will also provide comfort and support for both dog and owner in the terminal stages.

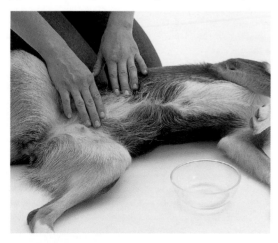
◁ If your dog can bear to have its tummy touched, an aromatherapy massage can provide some much-needed comfort.

Physical problems: first aid

Accidents will happen in the best run households. It is valid for an owner to give first aid, but any dog involved in a serious accident must always be checked by a vet. Complementary medicines are well suited for first aid use in the home.

artificial respiration

The routine for attending to injured dogs is essentially the same as for a human. If it is not moving check to see if it is conscious by pinching the web between its toes; a conscious dog will pull its foot back. If it doesn't, watch to see if the chest is moving. If it is, the dog is breathing, if it isn't make sure that there is no blood, mucus or other material obstructing the throat and nose. If it does not start to breathe, hold the dog's mouth closed and blow gently down its nose and watch its chest rise as air enters the lungs. Keep the lungs inflated for the count of three and then let the air out naturally. Repeat this at five to ten second intervals. In between puffs, feel for a heartbeat with your fingers on the ribs just behind the elbow. If there is no beat, cardiac massage can be

given by squeezing the chest vigorously between the fingers and thumb of one hand once or twice a second. Alternate the breathing and squeezing, changing every 15–20 seconds. If there is no heartbeat in four minutes, the heart is unlikely to restart. Artificial respiration can be kept up for 20 minutes if there is a heartbeat.

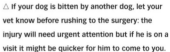

△ If your dog is bitten by another dog, let your vet know before rushing to the surgery: the injury will need urgent attention but if he is on a visit it might be quicker for him to come to you.

bleeding

If there is serious bleeding, put a layer of wadding (batting) material over the wound and then apply a firm bandage. A conscious dog may well object to being handled and it may be necessary to tie a piece of bandage, such as a tie or scarf, around its mouth to stop it biting you. If the vet hasn't been told before, tell him now and arrange to take the dog to the surgery. The first aid treatment for shock that accompanies any accident is either to give two drops of the Bach Flower *Rescue Remedy*, or a tablet of homeopathic *Aconite 6C* or *30C*. These medicines can be given to unconscious dogs because they will be absorbed through the mouth lining.

◁ Small bites can be bathed with diluted hypercal tincture before they are dressed. If the wound is gaping, stitches will be needed.

wounds

Cuts and bruises result from many causes. If necessary, treat for shock and bleeding, as above. In addition, homeopathic *Arnica* is the ideal medicine for all cuts and bruises, although if the bruising is severe, change from *Arnica* to *Bellis perennis* after a couple

Fight wounds and road accidents are always accompanied by a degree of shock. Always give either Rescue Remedy or Aconite before doing anything else. Minor wounds can be cleaned and dressed before seeing a vet. If there is a lot of bleeding, use thick padding and bandage as firmly as the dog will allow.

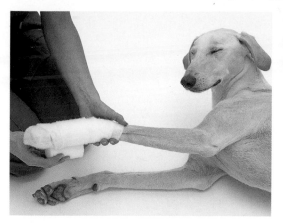

△ **1** Having removed any objects from the wound and after cleaning it, apply a bandage to cover it, using a non-stick dressing and a soft cotton bandage. It may need two people: one to comfort the dog, the other to treat it.

△ **2** In an emergency, masking tape or adhesive tape may be used instead of elastoplast to hold the dressing in place. Take the adhesive bandage 3cm (1in) up the fur to prevent it from slipping off.

of days. *Hypericum* helps for crush injuries to the legs and tail, and *Calendula* is good for minor cuts, and grazes. If the bleeding persists, give *Phosphorus* or *Ipecacuana* to stop it, and *Hamamelis* stops dark-coloured oozing from badly bruised wounds. Use the *6C* potency of all homeopathic remedies.

Acupuncture can help relieve severe pains. The tissue salt *Ferrum phos.* can stop bleeding if a powdered tablet is sprinkled on the wound, and can also be given by mouth afterwards. Minor wounds can be

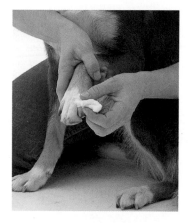

△ **Wounds between the toes and on the sole need to be dressed. They will gape as the dog walks, allowing dirt to enter.**

cleaned with *Hypercal* tincture diluted 1:10 and *Hypercal* cream used as a dressing. Essential oils of *Lavender* or *Terebinth* may be massaged around wounds, but must not be put on them directly. Serious wounds must always receive professional help.

burns and scalds

These are caused by dry and moist heat respectively and can be very painful. Do not put grease on them but bathe them with cold water. Bach Flower *Rescue Remedy* and homeopathic *Aconite* can be given as for bleeding, and *Cantharis* will help, particularly if there is blistering. The surrounding area can be massaged with essential oils of *Lavender* and *Rosemary*.

bites and stings

Rescue Remedy and *Aconite* can be given if shock is suspected. Aromatic *Lavender* oil can be massaged around, but not on animal bites. Homeopathic remedies used are: *Arnica 6C* for dog bites that tear the skin and muscles; *Ledum 6C* for cat bites causing deep penetrating wounds which are more painful than they look; *Apis mel. 6C* for insect stings that are swollen, red, and better for cold bathing, while *Urtica urens 6C* works on stings that are better for warmth. These can be given every ten minutes if needed.

heat-stroke

This is usually seen in summer in dogs that have been left in cars or fallen asleep in bright sunshine, and it kills many dogs each year. The Bach Flower essence *Rescue Remedy* can be given initially. Among the homeopathic remedies *Belladonna 6C* given every five minutes will help dogs that can still stand and whose pupils are widely dilated; *Glenoine 6C* is more helpful if the dog has collapsed with an unnaturally high temperature. Contact your vet for conventional support, which includes fluid therapy and oxygen. Do not cool the dog too quickly as this can cause shock and make things worse. Cool the dog gently using tepid water on its ears and limbs.

poisoning

If poisoning is suspected you must seek veterinary help immediately. If the dog has swallowed human tablets let the vet know the name and quantity of the tablets swallowed. Do not try to make the dog vomit unless advised to do so by the vet. You can begin by giving the Bach Flower *Rescue Remedy*, followed by *Crab Apple* for detoxification. Homeopathic *Nux vom.* also helps detoxification, and *Veratrum alb.* can be given if the dog is cold and collapsed, especially if it also has diarrhoea.

The death of your dog

No being, human or animal is immortal. The cycle of birth, life and death is natural and unbreakable. It will always be completed. Many people who are interested in complementary health take the view that the essential spirit of the organism continues to exist after the death of the physical body, perhaps rejoining with an invisible source from which all life manifests. Whatever the case, in due time it will be your responsibility that the transition from life to death is as easy and pain-free as possible for your dog.

Most owners hope that when that time comes for their dog to die it will do so peacefully in its sleep, or they will be there to comfort it. Often dying is protracted however. It is then the owner's task to decide if and when to euthanase their pet in order to relieve it from suffering.

Many owners find this an extremely difficult decision, and will ask their vet for advice. I would ask any owner faced with this situation to consider their relationship with their dog as a two-way contract. They have undertaken to give their dog a good life, to care for it and to protect it. In return, the dog has rewarded them with the pleasure of its company. When the stress of nursing the pet is having an adverse effect on the health of its owners, or if the dog is suffering from incurable pain, then euthanasia should be considered. Vets are qualified to say when they think the suffering is too much for the dog to bear, but they cannot know how the owners are feeling or how family life is being affected. The owners must decide when to end the partnership and usually they know when that time comes.

Even at this sensitive time, holistic care can help both dog and owners. The Bach Flower *Walnut* helps humans and animals cope with difficult changing circumstances and can help with the stress of dying. Homeopathic *Arsen. alb.* given in rising potencies helps to dispel the fear of dying that many feel towards the end of a long terminal illness. *Ignatia* is a good remedy for grief and can be given to the dog's owners to help them adjust to, and accept, their loss. If their grief seems never-ending, *Natrum mur.* will help them finally come to terms with their loss.

◁ **Life and death are two sides of the same coin but it does not make parting with an old friend any easier.**

▷ **Your dog's last days should be as happy as the rest of its life. Holistic treatment throughout its life will help to achieve that end.**

Useful Addresses

UNITED KINGDOM
Association of British
Veterinary Acupuncture
East Park Cottage
Handcross
Haywards Heath
West Sussex RH17 6BD

Association of Chartered
Physiotherapists in Animal
Therapy (ACPAT)
Morland House
Salters Lane
Winchester
Hampshire SO22 5JP
Tel: (01962) 844 390

The Bach Centre
Mount Vernon
Bakers Lane
Brightwell-cum-Sotwell
Oxfordshire OX10 OPZ
www.bachcentre.com

British Association of Homeopathic
Veterinary Surgeons (BAHVS)
The Alternative Veterinary
Medicine Centre
Chinham House
Stanford-in-the-Vale
Oxfordshire SN7 8NQ
www.bahvs.com

British Holistic Veterinary
Medicine Association (BHVMA)
The Croft
Tockwith Road
Long Marston
North Yorkshire YO26 7PQ
Tel: (01743) 261 155

McTimoney Chiropractic
Association (MCA)
Crowmarsh Gifford
Wallingford
Oxfordshire OX10 8DJ
www.mctimoneychiropractic.org

UNITED STATES
American Holistic Veterinary
Medical Association (AHVMA)
PO Box 630
Abingdon, MD 21009-0630
www.ahvma.org

International Veterinary
Acupuncture Society (IVAS)
1730 South College Avenue
Suite 301
Fort Collins, CO 80525
www.ivas.org

International Association for
Veterinary Homeopathy (IAVH)
Susan G. Wynn, DVM
334 Knollwood Lane
Woodstock, GA 30188
www.iavh.org

American Veterinary
Chiropractic Association (AVCA)
442154 E 140 Road
Bluejacket, OK 74333
www.animalchiropractic.org

Academy of Veterinary
Homeopathy (AVH)
PO Box 232282
Leucadia, CA 92023-2282
www.theavh.org

CANADA
Canadian Veterinary Medical
Association
339 Booth Street
Ottawa
Ontario K1R 7K1
www.canadianveterinarians.net

Ontario Veterinary College
University of Guelph
50 Stone Road
Guelph
Ontario N1G 2W1
www.ovc.uoguelph.ca

AUSTRALIA
Balmain Village Veterinary Clinic
11 Beattie Street
Balmain
NSW 2041
www.balmainvillagevet.com.au

Glen Osmond Veterinary Clinic
308 Glen Osmond Road
Fullarton
SA 5063
www.glenosmondvet.com.au

Greencross Vets Forest Lake
447 Waterford Road
Ellen Grove
QLD 4077
www.greencrossvet.com.au/
Clinic-4/Forest-Lake.aspx

Acknowledgements

The author and publisher would like to
thank the following for their help and
advice in the production of this book:
Anna Brown, Jane Burton, Fiona Double-
Day, Carmen Fernandez, Kay McCarroll,
Stuart Macgregor, Carolyn, Catherine
and Peter Richards, Britta Stent and
Narelle Stubbs. And not forgetting…
Alec, Alfie, Bertha, Bess, Brak, Fan,
Gemma, Henry, Jack, Jorge, Lark, Mandy,
Molly, Muppet, Patch, Rio, Rosie, Sam,
Sky, Solo, Sophie, Swift, Tansy and Tiggy.

Index